SWALLOWING
THE WORLD

NEW AND SELECTED POEMS

SWALLOWING
THE WORLD
NEW AND SELECTED POEMS

BY DON FREAS

Lost Arts Design
Olympia, WA

SWALLOWING
THE WORLD
NEW AND SELECTED POEMS

BY DON FREAS

www.DonFreasPoetry.com

ISBN 978-0-9725074-6-2

Library of Congress Control Number: 2015904981

Cover and book design by Debi Bodett
www.DebiBodett.com

Printed in the United States of America

First Edition
Published by Lost Arts Design
Olympia, Washington

ACKNOWLEDGMENTS

A version of "Wild Love" first appeared in *Portland Review*; "Sketch" was previously published in *Rosebud* Magazine; "She is Almost" appeared in *Bellowing Ark*; and "Five Haiku" was published by *Asheville Poetry Review*. Many thanks to these and other journals and magazines that have published my poems.

Several of my many teachers need to be named here—Robert Bly, for opening my ears and heart to poetry—and for asking for a copy of my first poem. Coleman Barks, for releasing Rumi into American English. Liam Rector, for being so completely Liam Rector; I miss you.

Speaking of Liam—my eternal gratitude to the Bennington Writing Seminars: poetry, writing, and so much more. The convocations were truly transformational.

I can't possibly name all the characters and groups that have helped shape these poems through workshops, critique groups, and writing groups over the last 25 years. You know who you are. Your careful reflections have been greatly appreciated. Thank you.

Fans of my poetry—you have no idea how much it means when you tell me what you like, respond openly to particular poems at readings, or write to point out how you have been touched by the poems. It can be such an isolating practice, alone with a pen and paper, or a keyboard. Don't get me wrong, I love creating alone, but your comments, laughter, tears, and sighs—and the moments when I look up in the middle of a poem to find the whole audience listening in eyes-closed contemplation—with these you let me know something comes through. Thank you.

Finally, and always, Debi Bodett—not only for making this book so beautiful for me, but for everything else. Thank you.

CONTENTS

Section 2 / Waiting Room

Section 3 / In Place

Section 4 / Traveler

Section 5 / Now

PREFACE

A poem on the page is a script for an event that hasn't happened yet. It's an invitation to an ephemeral experience that comes to life when you lift the poem from the page with your eyes, and mix it with your awareness, phrase by phrase. As attention drops down the ladder of lines, something mysterious accrues. You can feel it.

Poetry originated well before the written word, as a spoken art. To carry, a poem had to be memorable. The sound and sense of a poem naturally became concentrated, spare, compelling— or it was soon forgotten. When you pick a poem that you find intriguing, and say it aloud, the experience releases that timeless intensity. What you hear changes as the sounds resonate and return to your ears and mind. Those nearby can feel it too.

You can rely on a poem. A good poem comes along with you, the meaning changing as you evolve through the vagaries of experience. Of course, not just any poem will do. Finding the poems that hold you steady amid the profusion can be like look-ing for sea shells, beach glass, or fossil shark teeth by the ocean. Keep your eyes open—your poems will find you.

Visit a few poems over and over; let them vibrate in your chest. Or collect and consider a great many poems. The practice is clarifying; you can know yourself.

SWALLOWING
THE WORLD
NEW AND SELECTED POEMS

Being Human

NATURAL HISTORY

You lean toward me and the first pebble
tumbles from my summit. Encouraged,
you express love for my forests, and fire
sweeps my flanks, making weeks of smoke
and releasing the tree people from
long-standing triumph. Erosion follows.
I resist, wanting to remain as I was:
settled, remote. You send glaciers
to etch my slopes, rain and wind
by the millennium to flay me to bone.
Steadfast I remain a barren pinnacle
shedding rocks day by day, your love
pulling, demanding. The explosion
of my birth so long ago begins to feel
like so much artifice. I lean toward you
and watch as my faces peel away in slabs
that crumble into outpourings of dust.
You take me again and again, your love
endless. I lay out in sweeping moraines
over the fields, watch myself become
the gentle, undisturbed horizon.
Still you pull and rivers carry me
far from the solitary upthrust I was
when I first met your desire.

CONFLUENCE

It was no surprise that her waters
were so clear as to be invisible,
or that his were nearly opaque,
thick with mud—though he
never would have admitted it.
The surprise was that they attracted
one another. They appeared to have
no basis for communion, no way
to relate: she ran from the mountains,
he from the fields. Still, their ways
kept pouring them into one cut.
Both knew downhill was essential,
so they didn't eddy long before
going on. Intermittent rapids challenged
their natural differences. Where they
mingled, he gained clarity—
his browns went polished amber,
even blues arose, translucent.
And she became visible—
what had passed undetected
now gathered form: her smoky curves
wafted through, compounding the beauty
of their course, drawing attention.
She learned to love the glance;
he to relish revelation.
They recognized themselves
in the water of one another,
and the mixture suited them both
all the way downstream.

WHOLE TIME

The opposite of shadows is not light
but the reflection in her eyes
by the pond that afternoon in spring.
Up close I could see white ducks,
new cattails, and ash trees round-topped
on the far side. Even the sky: the whole
world laid itself open to study over
the polished slate of those obsidian pupils;
two worlds slightly different ringed
by her nutbrown irises. She turned
from my stare, smiling, embarrassed,
and took all reflection with her until
I coaxed and kissed her enough that she
opened up and brought those liquid worlds
back to gaze at me. I can't believe she's
ninety now, and that we've been together
since we were kids. Sometimes in the mirror
I don't know who I'm looking at. Sometimes
she whispers "Who are you, old man; and
what have you done with my beau?" I wink
at her, and tease back watching
for my own eyes in the twinkle
over faded hazel
I've known forever.

KINDLING

In St. Augustine, my father
and I learned to make fire
from a spark thrown
by the forceful glance of stone
on steel. We learned
how to catch the spark
in a nest of char-cloth, how
to feed our soft breath
to the embedded ember until
it became a small tongue
of flame. With care,
that flame could be fed
in turn to a handful
of Spanish moss, dried
to receive the blessing lick.
Twigs followed, then sticks,
then staves split from oak.
We were enthralled,
Dad and I. The young man
who taught us made fire
each day this way, to heat
his forge. He dressed
in homespun clothing,
with a leather pouch
that held the fire kit
on his belt. The pouch
was handmade as well,
by other craftsmen nearby.
The blacksmith seemed to be
more comfortable
in another age. In the light of his
easy passion, I wondered
if any of us truly fits
this disjointed world,

where we are unhooked
from fabrication of the simplest
things—the fires in our homes
cycling on and off
with electronic timers
and valves beyond our reach,
stabilizing the weather
without a thought—
even the gas payment now
automatic. I've heated
a home with wood fire,
warmed twice by hauling-in
eight cords a winter,
and I do not long
for what's been called,
strangely, a simpler time.
But I am still fascinated
by the essential making
of things, the magic
transformation of one form
into another: hot iron under
a hammer, becoming a hinge;
a gathering of iron, rock, charred
cloth, and breath to contrive
light and warmth—the way
sparks flew, gentle blowing into
cradled hands, the tiny lick
of flame; my father and me
kindling fire.

ALL THAT REMAINED, STILL SINGING

There was lightning on my birthday night. We saw it
over toward Gettysburg, just before the sky went dark,
violent and silent. The intensity was such that we wondered
if a late display of Fourth of July fireworks was underway.

But the growl slowly rose, and wind brought the storm to us
as if to stay. Bursts of light came from inside the night air
above us, bolts so bright they sparked sudden visions
of hot green fields, and folded forest hills, in hard detail.

Then it came from the south, behind hills, tracing
their round tops in silhouette. It was as if an army
were passing near, intent on other populations worthy
of their expenditures. Their black mass flowed

down the valley, and we worried they might make camp
nearby for the night. Overhead, we saw jagged forks travel
from cloud to cloud, and other clouds that pulsed
with inner explosions going nowhere. For hours our eyes

fielded the intensity. My father held a flashlight ready
for the likelihood of electrical failure; my mother made us
move our chairs back from the big windows, and told
what she had heard about people who survived strikes.

The storm remained so long, and was so strange,
that we went silent, and sat alone together watching—
our chairs clustered back to back in the center of the room.
We watched as if this were the final fire, as if we would

now live always in the shade of explosion and immolation,

as if this had become the condition of the world. All our plans
and patience—the very future—sat stunned to a frozen,
adrenaline doze. We wondered from our own small spheres

about the bridges and roads, and what it would take
to get to market. We wondered if we would have to live
always ready to dodge, and grieve steadily, and gather
bitter water running, with only a hint of red,

from the battlefield. But finally the cannons rolled on.
We couldn't tell if anything was left. Other than a single
streetlight—a picket's lantern burning on the far hill—
all that remained, still singing.

AFTER DARK

When fire was still precious,
and electricity belonged to lightning,
darkness held the night, and we
would lie down at dusk to avoid

stumbling into things.
In the higher latitudes, in winter,
we would be in bed for more hours
than we needed sleep.

I'm told we lived a pattern
of sleeping half the night, then waking
in the middle to talk—
processing dreams and the day—

then more sleep would ensue,
until first light when we could
see our hands again, and put them
to use. It sounds romantic, but

it feels true—especially when,
after a few hours of sleep, we both
wake and talk for awhile. I can
feel then how sorely I've missed

the raw silk of those low voices,
lips near to ears, the world
drawn in by absence of vision
to a cozy nutshell, warm

and delicious, where we can be
held close for awhile, when
there is nothing else to do.
The thrill I feel as I listen

to your small night voice
reminds me: I hold
my breath to catch
every whisper.

KISSTORY

brotherly kiss
stolen kiss
prairie highway kiss
draw you into me kiss
couch kiss
wish I could kiss
back to husband kiss
phone kiss
I'll be free kiss
post divorce kiss
free at last kiss
all the way kiss
full body kiss
river-running kiss
marry me kiss
anytime kiss
office supply kiss
passionate public kiss
honeymoon kiss
valentine kiss
home from work kiss
some time for us kiss
too tired kiss
why kiss
blank stare kiss
ex kiss
one more time kiss
friendly kiss
cool kiss
no kiss

Swallowing the World ◆ Don Freas

REUNION

I climbed up
behind you
into the big
sweatshirt you wore
slithered my arms
in the sleeves by yours,
my head
screwed through
the neckhole
another shadow
in the hood
behind you.
Walking was
awkward
at first, and we
had difficulty
deciding what our arms
would do. Verbal
deals had to be made:
"Can we
scratch my head?" "Part
of us has to pee."
After so much
            distance
being close
takes practice.

GATEKEEPER

Everything is ready, everything complete.

From the smoking remains, Janus
uses the bronze-shod heel of his staff to stir up
a few bits of charred bone, a smoke-occluded ruby,
twisted metal bands. He keeps one eye on the gate
as he draws a smooth skim of ash over the old firepit.
The creek chuckles in the draw. A storm-crow
sits the snag above the empty approach-trail.

There will be more pilgrims—coming and going—
some ready, some not. He knows what to look for,
what to ask. Beyond the gate everything is in order.
With a thought he makes the portal vanish,
then reappear. He moves back to the barrier
and leans his long body into the presence and patience
of a great oak. The world continues to revolve, stars

returning to locations abandoned long ago.
Everything complete. And ready.

BEFORE MY MOTHER

Pelicans fold wings and dive
for sardines between the surfers.
A spiny pufferfish has washed up

on the sand. Rain and cold at home
but this is January in Mexico—
my daughters and I, first day

of a long-awaited week together.
We wander the beach, then settle
on some rocks beneath a shady tree—

overwhelmed by the warmth, sun
and sand, and the sounds that arise
where ocean meets land.

We're there a long time—slowing
from travel, uncoiling swirls
of occupation and creation—

taking it in, easy, grateful—
the first full day away. In a while,
looking around, we notice

a big bird, perched on a limb, not far
above us in the tree. It's one of those
graceful magnificent frigate birds—

a female. Her elegant tail-feathers
curve down below the branch,
sharp wings folded in. Her head

is up, long beak pointing out
toward the rolling sea.
She remains still so long we all feel

some foreboding. Dozens of other
seabirds feed and tussle, squawk
and call, as nearby fishermen

gut their catch and throw back
the spoils. The frigate bird
seems to be in contemplation,

looking far, far out. Then she
moves—a few steps sideways
along the branch. Our hopes

rise a little. Maybe she's
a meditative bird, taking a break—
maybe they do this; we don't know.

But she comes to a stop, lowers
her wings to hang draping
around a fork in the branch, lays

her breast into the crotch, and dies.
No shudder, no quake, no sigh—
no other witnesses. Speechless,

stunned, honored—the three of us
look at one another, look back up.
We have been given a death.

With no clue as to what it might mean,
we hold the gift as sacred. A breeze
moves the long hanging feathers—

wing and tail. Sounds of surf, play,
camaraderie, continue without pause.
In a while we drift toward dinner,

but visit each day, wondering.
Sky burial, breeze in the feathers,
a few begin to fall. One week later,

in Florida, my mother
doesn't see the truck,
pulls out.

TAKING HER BODY

Every half minute her body
gathers strength to draw one

or two more shallow
breaths. She hasn't eaten

in two weeks and now takes
only the water we sponge

on her tongue. We can't
understand her whispers

and feel clumsy holding her
on the edge of the bed

where she tries to rise
on legs that can't

hold her anymore.
Unfinished, her body

animated by will, she
remains while we let go.

And outside, the Sun
eats itself as fast as it can.

WINDFALL

Wind gusts in the night shake down
hickory nuts by the hundreds—

each one hits the roof with a bang,
bounces, and falls to whack the deck.

Overlapping double-strikes become
an echoing golf-ball barrage, and

that chaotic two-strike "thunk,
thunk" makes a lullaby with jazz.

Morning light, all those fallen nuts
on the deck. I start to sweep them off

and find another amazing sound—
the rolling spheres raise a rumbling

cacophony on the old boards.
With rapid broom strokes I can keep

lots of hickory nuts rolling toward the edge.
The din dies quick when I let up, so I

sweep faster, lose myself in the sound
and flurry. Time stands still; the broom

dances, hickory nuts jump, and thunder.
The nut dance raises the whole mess

into song, a delicate tempest,
that glides over the salt marsh, smoke.

BURIAL

The hole through sod into the old
loam of the Appalachian hillside,

is about right for a fence post.
With nothing to lean on, my father

stands by the dark hole with tears
in his eyes. The wooden box holding

Mom's ashes is in there, as deep
as my brother and I could reach

without dropping it. Some tentative
letting go is scheduled for today.

They were married sixty years.
My father is lost, and will remain lost—

but he's tougher than he looks, more
resilient than he feels. Even lost,

the charm and kindness that attracted her
gets him by. There will be no going back

this time. His gaze rests on his own name
carved in stone by hers. "You'll all be

back here soon for me" he says.
Soon enough, here we are.

WARMTH

My father, dead a year,
woke me in the night—
he was cold, and couldn't sleep.

I swaddled his old, thin body
in my comforter, and slept
cold myself until dawn—

when I realized my father
wasn't there. I pulled
his fading warmth over me.

OUT OF ORDER

Crackers and tea, apples
sliced and browning, the hot drink
poured from a thermos. We had
a blanket, laid on soft gravel
and the river chuckled nearby.

She said "Which is worse,
to live beyond the suicide
of your child, or to live
your life the child
of a suicide?" It was not

an academic question. She
was seeking the rise of compassion
she might find in consideration
of another suffering more
than she. It didn't work—

not yet. She knows there is
no answer. All death leaves
tracks. Left behind, we consider
what will come for us—because
it will. History says only fools

imagine a proper order to
the fatal dance. Yet we proceed,
calculate in private, commiserate
over picnics, with crackers and apples—
dying all the while in our turn.

HONOR THY DAUGHTERS

Honor runs both ways. Through you
into a cramped world they came—an easy
choice that assures devastation. They reach out
their small arms to find walls, horrors,
along with unicorns of delight, and the pulse
of your dancing heart. Now they are

women in a boiling cauldron—hammered
and beguiled into their talents and unique grace.
They've learn to fight like girls, to glow like women,
to push back. Feel the terror, embrace
the inspiration. They dance among predators,
the bludgeons of love, the certainty of damage

to what cannot be damaged. They learn, they teach,
they fail, and flail. They weave beauty from flaws
to become themselves. Notice how they
live what you longed for, but could not have.
They don't know what you know: they know
what you don't. Fold at the waist, bow

to the mystery; let them make you more.
With any luck you will leave them orphaned
in a cruel land; suffer that now. Free them
to find their feet and build a world less cruel.
Pray they won't leave you here alone—
                                        trust that, when they do.

SHADOW

Three long blocks from home, evening—almost night.
He is out for a walk, and being shadowed by
a wolf. He has felt this wild presence before,

but this time he catches a glimpse between the trees
by the gully, and again as he turns the corner
at Sylvester and Thomas. There's an empty

lot there, overgrown. The wolf is very near, and silent.
She melts from one dark bush to another. He keeps his pace
and lets the hot tendril of fear snake through his body.

He wonders what the wolf is waiting for. She reads
his state and decodes signs for a cue. He notices
he's feeling tasty, and that seems like cause

for concern. He would fight the wolf for life
if he had to, but knows as well that he isn't
deathly afraid—it wouldn't be the first time

he has been consumed. He scans from side to side
watching for anything he can use as a club.
He begins a low whistle, some old hymn, as he listens

for the scrabble of a rush. Before long he comes
to his own driveway. He looks back with one foot
still in the road. The moon is a crescent—still up

just before the sky goes black. The stalker is watching,
but he can't see her now. He feels a strange,
familiar sadness, and thinks of going back.

But he knows the kids are inside.
They still need him; he can't shake the feeling
that the wolf knows that too. He turns

and goes to the door. He hears a faint rustle
in the brush, just before the door shuts tight.

TRAGEDY

My old friend and enemy—my brother
and most distant cousin—makes his visit,
as is expected. His son, in a rage,
had attacked me. In the fight that ensued,
I killed him. I had to kill him, or be killed.

My old friend and enemy enters my hall.
I have the hands and head of his son, packed
with honor, wrapped in linen, in a basket
with sheepskin cover—as custom dictates.
I don't want him to look; know he must.

Kneeling before the basket, my friend draws
one long breath, then folds back the cover.
With resolve and courage he peels back
bloody layers. I stand in witness.
He crumbles, forehead to floor, weeping.

When he's ready he stands, faces me.
We lock hands, then hold one another, shaking.
I say "If there had been some other way…"
He dismisses my sentiment. Ferocious,
we hold a silence so deep there is no bottom.

RACE

All they had done
was to be born to their mothers
of the blood of their fathers
and grow true from that, as they had,
to play basketball
in the old school yard
under the hill, where one day

three white boys, born
to their mothers, of their fathers,
came down the hill, through
the woods, and surprised even themselves
when they showed how true they'd grown
by yelling the triggering epithet.

That was enough, finally,
that they all boiled up the long hill,
basketball spinning to still on the tarmac,
one handful after the other
through the forest,
each carrying his own
delicate shard of the rage of ages;
skinny white legs howling

in the terror of what they had done
for no reason; hunters closing
on the quarry they'd been born
to hunt, ready to occupy
the hilltop and lay siege
for three days, awaiting
the chance for blood—
or an apology, then blood—
as if either would make a difference.

CONTRITION AND HUMILITY

First day on the job, I show up
in boots, tool belt hung over my shoulder.
There's a sandwich in my lunch box, coffee
in the thermos. About a dozen old hands
shake mine. The foreman says

"Let's get to it." The workers all turn
away from the concrete and stacks
of lumber. They line up in an arc along the rim
of a big mud pit; I take a place at one end.
Hands at our sides, or crossed in front,

eyes downcast, we hold the silence.
I'm thinking: *This is not like any crew*
I've been on. I look at the mud, wondering.
Then one guy shakes his head, says, "Yeah,"
and drops forward into a pushup, barehanded

in the mud. He gently lays himself full-face
in, and lets go. After a moment,
he works his way back up to standing.
A rough looking woman says "Shit, me too,"
and does the same. She gets up. We stand

another few minutes, silent—until the foreman
says "Ok, thanks." The line breaks and the crew
moves back toward the day's work. Seems like
more than the usual back-slapping ensues,
with exchange of good mornings, talk of families,

updated stories. The foreman grabs
some rags and takes them to the two
muddied volunteers. He wipes their faces

like a father might clean a child following
a messy breakfast. He says, just to them,

"Good work—We all needed that."
The woman says "I know I did." The man smiles
and says "Boy, howdy." They change into clean
coveralls, and gather their tools. Nail guns
and chop-saws begin to wail.

WHOPPER

I don't know who the visitor was—
child of friends of my parents, my age—
which must have been seven or eight.
I don't remember ever making up
such a lie as I told him. We were walking
down the nameless Ohio creek
in the woods below our house,
and by a familiar pool I began to tell
of the giant crayfish that had taken
my twin brother one day, while
we were playing by the water.
The beast just came up, grabbed
my brother, and then I was alone
forever. I nearly wept recalling
the imagined loss. I remember it
like I didn't care if he believed me,
like I wanted it to be real.
I surprised myself with the depth
of feeling, and wonder still
if I truly had another brother, taken
suddenly while young—because
even writing this I reach
for his name, his lost smile,
and I miss him.

BEING MULTIPLE

There are beings on this very planet
who have scattered themselves, blown open
the solo envelope, fractured generations beyond
the lonely container of separate contiguous skin.

In so doing they have stepped out of single
life cycle, and into abiding existence—standing
for thousands of years on their own husks.
We see it every day: flights of geese laughing

high above, the light-footed raccoon
with her three round babies dancing in tow;
salmon, breaking the water's surface one
by one, exhibiting their greater presence—

infused throughout the gathered liquid torso
of the bay—dispersed, yet still of one mind.
Step back and consider the flow of tree-beings
pouring their species across the landscape—

in patience breathing out forest on fallen
forest, casting forth seed to rise
and rise forever. Do you see it? Watch
a school of trout, nose upstream, holding

in the flow, or a rolling fog bank of shorebirds
folding back on itself. Soften your focus
to see the fine threads that align—what looks like
a group of individuals—into the one that is us.

SWALLOWING THE WORLD

This morning was orange before
the Sun drew itself up and in
from the flat quagmire of night
to form itself, gently,
into the day's necessary round ball.
Now we have the new day. Here
is the fullness, here is the space

to be filled with you, love,
and your calm. We have chores;
we live as other creatures do,
but in the morning I feel you
reach out into ferns,
into trees, into the pattern
of waves on the bay, into

the spray of light through mist
as if these were all you.
You feel your way as well
into the profusion of festivals and wars,
into the ninety-nine feasts and
quiet places of starvation, into
the thousands of suffering rapes

and the uncountable sweet couplings
of lovers. I watch the fleeting
weather of your face, as you squeeze again
through the birth canal, and breathe
again the long emptying exhale
of death. No wonder you go quiet
so often. No wonder you need to sit

by the window and watch the birds.
I see tears behind your smiles and know
there's nothing to say. I've made coffee;
you cup the cup in your clever hands,
inhale the fragrant steam.
We will have visitors; we will host
and laugh, as we do. But it is these

times alone I live for, when we un-form
and drop all pretense, find ourselves
not only in the beauty and good,
but equally in the horror that is earth.
I watch in awe as you flicker in and out
with the Sun's newly formed light
in your hair. I put my hand behind

your heart; you lean into me,
accept it all again, even understand
the world. The cup comes to your lips;
you sip, testing, tasting,
then take a full draw, swallow,
embrace again the only work
that truly needs to be done.

Waiting Room

REFLECTION

Sometimes they are only stunned—
so when I heard the WHAM!
that could only be *bird in flight surprised
by glass,* I went to see
if I could help. A little thrush lay
on the boards, a little blood
on the twisted beak, a tiny shudder
as she died. She had turned
toward a stunning illusion
of the world, and found it shallow
and inflexible. What appeared
to be air and open space was not;
what looked like vastness became
suddenly flat, and lethal, used
her own momentum against her.

The big window above us was
a perfect mirror, morning sun
deep in its crystalline repetition.
I could see white clouds,
sky pale morning blue, the Cascade
range and Mount Rainier—all
that the bird had perceived during
that last misjudged arc. Nearer
I saw my own aging figure,
with a limp, feathered ball
growing cold in my hand, even
the shine of eye, glisten of feather,
body held out like an offering.
I wanted her to come back to life,
but she did not respond to my desire.

WAITING ROOM

One woman has her knitting—
looks like a mitten. Another guy,
less prepared, leafs through
a magazine about fishing.
Must be three characters with
their smart-phones out, texting,
surfing, answering emails. All
pretty standard—until a man
comes in with a suitcase, signs
at the desk, and unpacks
tennis balls, a funny hat.
He juggles while waiting. He's good.
Several other people become
audience members—they
clap at the right times, cheer
the juggler on. One young man
looks around, then steps out
into the hall. The rest of us
keep knitting, juggling, reading.
More people arrive. Then the guy
who stepped out comes back
with a box of fruit, and chocolate.
He sets up a little shop along
the back wall, selling his goods.
A few individuals try out being
customers—even the juggler
takes a break and buys a candy bar.
The waiting room becomes lively.
Two sisters start a little newsletter,
circulated every hour, to inform
new arrivals about what's going on.
The shop keeper and the juggler
take out ads. Visitors begin offering
massage, counseling, used shoes.

There's a yoga class at half past.
A team of carpenters knocks out
a wall to double the space. There is
some pressure to form government
but no one falls for that. People
coming and going. Most of us
have forgotten why we're here.
Someone will call for us,
one by one.

AFTER THE SAMBA

the men sweep the floor
and search the sweepings
to be sure
none of the silence
has been lost.

OUT WALKING TO SCHOOL

One morning I was walking to school
With books   out walking to school
Dry leaves all over   frosty morning
Walking the street down to school

Along the way was the woods
I always walk through the woods
Tall trees empty   brush by the trail
Through the woods to school

Walking among trees   there was sound
In the direction I'm walking   a sound
My ears lean toward it   the sound becomes louder
The sound through the woods toward school

The sound was garbled   honking
Unsure I was gentle   walking
Moving watchful   right at the sound
I came to the edge of the trees

The sound was nearby to the edge
The edge was the edge of grass
Cut grass a field sloping down
Down the slope far away   school

You could see the school there but I didn't
My eyes were too busy afield
Because in the field were geese
Hundreds of geese were there   *Hundreds*

The geese made the sound I'd heard
All together the sound in my ears
The chuckling talking sound
Sound filling my ears

I didn't know geese could be there
I'd never seen geese in that grass
It was great the geese on the way
The geese were the greatest thing ever

I liked to hunt as a boy
The geese made me think about hunting
My boy body wanted to figure a way
To kill and eat one of the geese

They rose from the grass all at once
The geese flapped and honked and rose up
The sound became huge I was enthralled
The geese I surprised flew away

I walked on to school with those hundreds
Of geese rising up in my eyes
Hundreds of geese honking and flapping
Filling the air in my eyes

I can still see those geese rise
I can still hear those geese talk
With eyes open I can go there
There's not much of school I remember

Now I was wanting a goose
All day I planned taking a goose
The next day I woke myself early
I woke up before anyone

My brother was asleep   I got up
Everyone asleep   I was up
I had my plan   I could see it
I got my bow and my arrows

Swallowing the World ◆ Don Freas

In my eyes the arrow would fly
The geese in the field in my eyes
The arrow would tip and come down
Quick the arrow would fall

The geese thick on the ground
in the grass where the geese were before
My arrow couldn't miss a goose in that crowd
The geese would all fly   save one

In my eyes that one would be mine
My goose would stay on the ground
My goose would be dead in my eyes
There was blood in my eyes

With my bow I walked down the street
Early morning I walked into the woods
My arrow ready   bow in my hand
The only sound going   my feet

Leaves made a noise from my feet
The geese might be hearing I thought
Slowly I moved through the woods
Quiet   came to the edge

Past trees   the big field of grass
In my plan the geese would be there
But no geese gaggled and laughed in the grass
No geese   not even mine

My arrow flew up and tipped
Falling   it stuck in the ground
I pulled out the arrow and walked
With only my eyes to eat

I never met geese there again
There may never *be* geese again
Each time I walk I listen
I still walk to school every day

CIDER TIME

A mess of crows have taken over
the driveway. They've eaten too many
fermented pears, and curse one another
as they teeter about the blacktop
fighting over mushy halves of fruit.
A few have carried their spoils to the roof,
where they roll half-eaten pears thumping
down the slope, then howl and cackle
as ragged carcasses vanish
over the gutter, and smack the deck below.
Now they are pounding on the chimney cap
like carpenters too happy
after a hard day and a couple of beers
to knock off and go home. The party
continues all afternoon. Crows come
and go, swallowed by their shadows.
Finally I notice silence and go out to deal
with the aftermath. Nothing I treasured
is missing, no real damage—broken fruit,
stray feathers, a lost pearl.

PEAR TREE IN WINTER

The tree has thrown down
the last of its Asian pears. It's been
weeks since the crows finished
their drunken feast, and moved on
to other taverns. Now, leaves
stain the ground old copper,
slick and glistening after rain.

The snag that remains could be dead—
a rag on the hillside, a perch too low
for crows, firewood for one day, no more.
If we didn't know better
we'd call it finished, used-up,
destroyed by the effort of making
the golden fruit we ate daily

in October. I'd drop the tree,
make a cane from the trunk,
turn an urn, slice out enough small boards
for a cat coffin. We'd burn the rest,
be done. But we've seen this—
with time and Earth's oscillation
a day will come when from the roots

juice will rise to trip winter's crystal latch.
If we let it be, one evening a green flush
will hover so near the branch tips
we'll wonder if the long dark
has tricked us into imagining light
to lift the fog-soaked pall; and
there will come pears again, dangling.

SKETCH

She draws him while she waits
hoping he will find her,

reducing line and shadow
of his ever-changing form.

Staying busy waiting,
she finds her way near

and from a distance
reforms him on her page;

looks away if he looks her way
but always leaves a trace.

DIDN'T HAPPEN

He did not hit
a land mine with
the rear wheels
of the deuce-
and-a-half he was
not retrieving from
where it was not
in Cambodia—where
the platoon had not
left it when they
did not engage
the enemy, and were
not killed. He did not
slide around the dirt
road corner too fast,
speed governor not
broken off, survival
moving him at
seventy down oxcart
roads where he was
not trying to catch up
with his non-existent
equipment recovery
team, who were not
bringing back trucks
that had never been
in Cambodia.
He did lose hearing
in his right ear,
did not get his
fourth purple heart,
took no disability
pay, knows why
he was there, lives

still contributing
in a country that
can't afford to
acknowledge him,
needs to be right,
or quiet.

RENEWAL

I know how they feel, the big trees,
with their massive weight that barely sways,
even in a gale—scars, and broken limbs
so terribly far from cool ground—
so much dead wood wrapped in living skin
drawn thin. How sweet to fall, to complete,
to compete again with grass and beasts for height;
to be near dirt—insignificant, supremely flexible;
to shed the stalwart effort of six hundred years
and be a twig; to begin again each year
among digging hooves and claws, the shade made
by salal; to dodge leaf-eaters and vie for light;
to take any stray ray, anytime, and make of it
a banquet. Ah, to be shorn and torn down—
bring your big saws, bring cables. Take
from me the burden of this single weight;
take my meat and bones onto your many wheels,
and haul in open ground, broken loam, an easy dig
for new roots, pale shoots—light everywhere for all
that stand to any height. Let me be new again,
tender among the tangle of shattered branches,
nothing among nothing, perfect.

FULCRUM

On any morning lit by the Sun
light tips over the forest
into the sloping field on the far hill,
and splits it north to south
with a raggedy sawtooth line—
half in night's twilight, half
in daylight. The teeth are treetops
of the crowding woods; their shadows
rake slowly west to east across
the hay that holds the open ground,
as the Sun's path pries the light
down toward morning, over
the living fulcrum. I can
make out a doe and two fawns
on the shady side, in the last minutes
before light takes the whole of it. And
I should linger no longer over
coffee and the cardinals' morning dance.
But it goes so fast; the work will never
be done, and never seems to mind
waiting for that entrancing shadow
to melt back into the woods.
We need someone watching—
someone who can bear witness
to the beauty of common passages,
and testify.

AT THE CROSSING

The river isn't wide, but crossing
seems impossible—angry flood,
laden with silt. Legend names
a ford here, but there are no
visible stones; and our waded advance
nearly carried us away.

Awaiting inspiration we feast
on catfish and the last
of our bread. You sing your lullaby
twice to the night, watersound
beyond. It's then I remember
the old man years ago. We came
upon him dancing by the road alone
to music only he could hear. We watched
from the cover of trees—making fun
at first, then growing quiet.

    Sustained now
by his abandon, knowing
he still dances, we awaken
in morning light on the far shore.

TO MAKE RAIN

Begin with desire: make it tremendous.
Be certain your longing is apparent—dance
wildly, wave your arms, arouse curiosity.
Forget reputation; image is no concern.

Intend to become moist and fluid. Look toward
density; identify areas of highest concentration
and focus there: gather, encourage. Practice
containing the uncontainable; find ways.

Dilate and disseminate. Focus on isolated dampness
at the periphery. Herd and group, surround. Make
the elements aware of their nature and potential.
Stress the basic necessity, play up flow, and fall.

Mollify what seeks desiccation. Some want dryness:
dust to rise and settle, brittle splintering.
Offer alternatives, negotiate agreements, forge links.
Lightning may be an expedient, or wind: use them.

If you've waited, the first movements may be pained
and slow: plan for it. Be a core that patiently courts,
a center around which desires willingly cluster.
Orchestrate the passions: make them tremendous.

Now, gather all you can hold, and rise, dumping heat.
Commit *all* your resources; take a deep breath. Align
with water and become liquid. Shatter into countless
bundles arcing outward and beginning to fall.

Breathe out tension. Let go into life-giving descent.
Intend to soak, to feed, to add spring and bend.
Commit to sound and deepening color; remain bent
on malleability; wash away barriers and order: be rain.

THIEF

The Goddess always watches—
I've grown weary of holding back.
That one golden apple—so perfect,
so forbidden, so just out of reach.
I long to feel that sacred orb
heavy in my hand.
Finally I give in and run.
With one leap the longed-for prize
grazes my fingertips. A flying twist,
and that precious weight becomes
part of my own.
                    There is no future
in awaiting the guardian's response—
so I run for the forest, fueled by a rich
mix of ecstasy and terror. An hour,
a day, maybe a year later, I drop
to rest by a still lagoon. As my
breathing slows, I roll the amber apple
between my palms, admiring
its mirror surface. There is no greater
joy than this.
                    The dark pond
begins to boil, as the stolen fruit
fades to a point—and vanishes.
The Goddess rises swirling from
the obsidian water. "My brazen
thief," she says, "my compliments."
Frozen, I stare. She continues,
"Now that you have stolen yourself
back from yourself, I have more work
for you. Take my hand."
We walked together
into the new morning. I have not
looked back.

HER RESPONSE
after Rilke's "You Don't Know Towers"

You are so obvious, upstanding,
tower-proud. Your probing incursions
return seminal booty; and each soaring
rocket splash reduces the size of the world.
Stalking the walls, you wear the edge
with ceaseless passage; yet so much
remains unnoticed within, bridged
and foregone in your resolute stride
toward certainty. Do you know
where the brook cascades
through a copse of ash trees?
There is a meadow inside, awash
with asters and columbine in spring,
where curling leaves reign through autumn,
and falling icicles chime the deaths of winter.
Time spreads there free of commerce
with peddlers and enemies, time
to curl inward unbound, to ease
into this shell-held body.
You will know enclosure in me,
and wander mossy trails
to nowhere, that fork and tee
and simply end. Sink into the warmth
of hearth; part these endless
curtain folds. Let the heat
swell us, this song repeat us,
our fabric dark-soaked, sodden.
Fall back open-armed through
permeable walls toward far more
feeling than either of us alone could feel.

BEING TREE

Unfold and reach, stand reaching
toward light with one hand, dark
and water with the other. Turn,
focused on a nearby star
that flickers above threading the sky.

Study elders. Fit the shape
of light they leave; study height,
become it. Build a form to wrap
reaching; bend in wind day after day

to make a body that never tires.
Fit the terrain beneath, entwine roots
with others nearby. Throw small
pieces of yourself onto wind, into distance;

watch them mold their own shapes
in light that comes through you; watch
as you grow again in them. Channel wind;
we'll make a climate among us, the day

raised above us, morning and evening
between us, even at noon. We'll shelter together,
take rain and hail, hold ice and moss,
gather mist and light. We will stand still

longer than memory, until we've always been.
We'll become as visible as stone, shape a place
until we are the place—our memory holding
everything in sight. Some of us will sacrifice

before our time, roots tearing loose
before storms. Most, when we die,
will stand dead a hundred years;
when we fall the earth will tremble.

TIMING

I know the hunger of pause,
the ache to cross distance
in an instant. I know
the generator of separation.
I've lived through bolt-storms
of return, light licking
from my toes and fingers.
I have faith in the wait,
can hold silent and watch
for the coming moment when,
with you distracted, I can slip
this poem in your sketchbook,
where you'll find it later
surprising, and consider me
an exceptional ghost.

SHE IS ALMOST

Piñon trees drip sap on her car all night
and she loves it. She waits on the rim
savoring her descent, takes a last walk among
ponderosa and Jeffrey pine. Mountain
holly drags at her tanning shins while
her eyes fill with light filtered
through flight feathers of turkey vulture,
high above dried poles of agave blossom.
She's a long way from the old order of Albany
where jumbled brownstones and muggy streets
tangle and confine her aging childhood.
It's just a few miles more to where saguaro
raise their arms to people hillsides
and ocotillo float crooked fronds
across the pumpkin moon.
Just a few miles down from the Mogollon,
creosote gullies writhe, quiet by day,
alive at night with coyotes, butterflies,
and beguiling incense. Teddy bear and
jumping cholla plant innocent smiles
above the flowing curve of snake
and dry-country river. In the basin below,
sunhigh heatwaves flag and waffle
drydistant mountains; hills hover
with bones exposed. A little water
is precious, as we rattle over hot stones;
lightning in the distance prods
torn, soundless clouds.
She grows arid and spare, leans
willing toward the extravagance
of just enough. She's
almost home.

THANKSGIVING (Occupy This)

The autumn shroud lifted from the northern tier this morning,
for the first time in a month. High winds and heavy rains
down here along the shores have blown off every shred

of summer leaf, cleared loose limbs, and driven
fair-weather sailors back inside their boat houses—
stocked with solitude, beer, and worn playing cards.

We have battened down the terrain, tarped the tractor
and brush hog, raked the great leaves back to piles
off the trails, where we won't have to track-in

their slippery decay. We withdraw to our febrile lookouts,
hunker by well-stoked stoves, sip coffee, and peer out
through shifting mists, as grape-sized raindrops pelt the roof,

and pour down the final seaward yards of every runnel
and crease. Of necessity, our vision has been reeled-in,
lowered—focused close. So this morning we wake, surprised

to find the curtain drawn back by a blue-sky high, and there—
at a distance we had been forced to forget—the long,
crenellated backbone that is the western slope of the old

Olympic range cuts a brilliant swath, deepening
far into the northern horizon. Last seen as gray stone teeth, dry
and worn a month ago, they have used their seclusion

to draw in the blast, freeze the chill rainforest mist and spray,
and glaze ridge and couloir in a razor-edged patina, steady
and perfect, stately—draped for winter—with the highest

peaks almost too bright in their heavy capes and caps.
No one can pretend, now, we'll have a lasting reprieve.
No one is ready—because no one knows what to be ready for—

though many will argue for opinions of various shade.
There is a time to gather and shout "not this," with
no offer of cohesive solution—I'm down with that.

But somewhere, behind the cloud banks and heavy mist,
within the obscuring darkness, boney and dry high places
are cloaking themselves in new white garments. Have faith,

trust yourself, with no reserve. Forget beliefs—
they're too close-in to matter. Gaze wide-eyed at the effusive
beauty; dare yourself to see it everywhere—give everything.

THE INFINITE FORM OF ENOUGH

This candle burns with a flame so small
it offers a light-field smaller
than a postage stamp from Burma.
When set alight the flame grows to illuminate
a space no larger than an eye.

Lean in close—vision will come
only after you have given up hope
of seeing anything, a little while
after you wonder if your eyes are closed.

Take it. Such a light is useful for exploring
the inside of a matchbox, the twisting
back corridors of a heart,
or the tiniest tubers of soul—
in these realms a wider light might blind
the subtle visions you seek.

Follow closely the narrowest corridor, trace
the curves of the finest caverns,
where sound inverts to become place
and place has no distinction from memory.

A torch this small offers little heat,
enough to warm one thought,
and that only to a simmer;
but close-looking will warm you,
and may be the same as seeing all.

FIVE HAIKU

Snowfall becomes full.
Forest trees wander hillsides
mumbling. They drift

with us toward open
air by river's edge, to bathe
their toes in motion.

Boulders painted with
frozen rivermist gather
glowing hats of white.

So steady the fall
it seems *we rise.* Trees and
river flow with us

upward toward some
other fate. Weightless we change
purpose to place, ascend.

PERSISTENCE

These first words, so
boring, so familiar—so much so
that I don't even want to say them again.

I am committed, though,
and spill them into the trough,
to watch as they burn, to add more:

"you again," "and you."
And in the heat and light—no...
under, behind, despite the light and heat—

something new emerges to ask
that I love the soil, too—the seed
and seedling as well as the fruit.

ART OF LEARNING

As the students come in I attempt
the usual friendly banter. A few engage;
I'm curious that many look away.
Recognition dawns when I notice
most are carrying hand-sized rocks.

I see it coming, so I name it:
Oh, you're here to stone me, I say.
I feel a little weary with the scene. But any teacher
who thinks he knows what he's really teaching
should look for other work.

I drop my hands to my sides
and turn away, inviting
the future. One stone hits the wall
over in the corner. Then another
drops to the floor. I hear a growing

clatter as dozens of falling stones
rattle on the concrete. I draw a breath
of gratitude—and wait for quiet. When I
turn back, I see that teachers
have replaced my students.

Okay, I say—*any further comment, questions?*
I let that hang a moment.

No?   Now, where were we. . .
as if any among us knows.

NOBLE TAPESTRY
for Tess

A quiet grove, aspens, on a hillside.
You enter, and find a proud golden thread
of sap running down the bark of one
breeze-shivering tree. It seems to be

of little consequence, until you follow—
and you will—and it will circle the world
leading you, leaving a backtrail you'll
never need, until it brings you, singing,

over the ridge again to this
same aspen grove. Eyes lined, hair
tied, soles worn thin as fallen leaves,
you'll remember, and laugh, smelling

the green drift of scent, foot-feeling
stones and pounded earth, bird song
filling your fatal cradle. One drop
then another weaving the same promise.

BEGINNING OF THE END

It was a long walk and we became
hungry. There was ripe fruit on a tree;
we ate, were satisfied, and walked on.

Farther along we were hungry
again. There was no tree with fruit.
We remembered the tree behind us

and wished it were here. There was
a stream and we drank. Fearing
there would not be another stream

we contrived a way to carry water
with us. And when we came to
another tree, we not only ate our fill

but carried fruit for our next hunger,
and wondered if we should bring the tree.
That pretty much explains everything.

In Place

SOLSTICE REPORT FROM RAIN COUNTRY

Wind moans over roof peaks, and plays bare branches.
Rain slaps the stove pipe cap like handfuls of sand,
then settles to an even tap over the lick and crack
of fire. New fallen water baptizes rocks, crows,
old bones, and rhododendrons, and chuckles
down the burgeoning draw. Having taken all it can,
the ground goes liquid, and flows. Houses—
built in wrong places—ride great gouts of mud
down toward the Sound, tearing loose
mooring pipes and cables, landing ruined
in the leveling tide. More blessing than we need,
this rain, to keep forests green and aquifers full.
But who has the temerity to damn prosperity
and risk the ensuing lack? We have raincoats
and broad-brimmed hats. Under a sweater,
hands in gloves, the fire inside proves us
more resilient than this ever-sloughing shore.
As the edge gives way, we can step back,
take a perch more stable. This is what is born
again in winter: the side-step that checks
our slide, the promise of a foundation
set below the reach of rain, a vessel
with deepened keel rigged for storm and song.
No one can give us this gift. We each split
our own from the dry heart, kindle the blaze,
huddle close. Listen carefully with every sense
and there will be no trick to knowing
when to take a step, or which way—
any course forward through this squall.

AS IF THESE WERE YOU

Submit to the rising star, as it bores through trees
on the ridge across the bay, only to wink out again
behind clouds.
        Submit to colors that fall
into the puddle you can see from the window.
Let that reflection call you out of the house
to find the sundog that will grow in time
to become a rainbow.
        Submit to the falcon
that backstrokes the air and throws
his taloned feet up to land on the rail
of your porch. Let him consume your heart
as you consume his eyes.
        Submit to the warbling
voice of the vireo that haunts the same bend
in the trail all summer, and to the day she is silent.
Give in especially to the silence.
        Submit to the call
to create; and through making learn the meaning
of failure. Gather mistakes as if they were
raw diamonds, as if you could never
have enough.
        Submit to the raven who stirs grumbling
from his roost at first light, to find you already up
and passing through his domain. Listen well to catch
the difference in the sounds of airflow
over wing and tail.
        Submit to a morning of stillness
seated on a piñon hill above the canyon's mouth.
Observe the rituals of local denizens: the pattern
of wren activities, the doe who finds her morning bed
and reads the whole valley with care before
she settles in; let your eyes find the mountain lion

that yawns in a clearing on the next hill. When
it's time to go, you'll know.

Submit to the insistent
human call that comes to you in a dead language
echoed down the centuries—only you will hear it,
and you will only hear it once. When you can't
interpret the words, grasp the feeling—gather their
ancient intent; comply as if all life depended on you,
as if you knew just what to do.

Submit to
the canyon rim. Trace it far enough to find
the Anasazi camp tucked under the edge. Follow
their fine ramp to the canyon floor and the stone
water tank that still fills with every storm. Consider
what was stored here for you.

Submit to the lightning
that comes, to the storm that stays until the whole
world seems to be broken open, and beyond repair.
Embrace the wreckage that remains.

Submit to aging,
to illness, to loss, and grief, unto death.
Submit to what is most difficult:
to joy and release.

Submit to whatever is now,
to this poem, to the delicate light on stones,
to your companions breathing,
to your own breath,
to nothing else.

PENNSYLVANIA FARM

Our neighbor Miller thinks in acres
and talks like water while his sprayer fills
from the clear flow of Muddy Creek.
I could listen all day to his easy drawl
and resonance, if he could talk so long.

I doubt it. He has work to do—new
spells to cast: spray and fertilizer timing,
extension agent shamanism, chemical
company voodoo. It works:
Miller's quilt on the far hill holds

green soybeans patchworked with long rows
of corn, blankets of alfalfa. First light to last
he times his progress over brown soil
and deepening green, this hollow and the next,
precious hilltop flatland, the steeper slopes

between—long-managed for timber, winter
heat, and boundary. County roads follow
hollows: flood in spring, freeze in winter.
A lattice of forest roads carries old tractors,
clashing threshers, plows, balers and rakes,

the occasional farm kid on dirt bike, hunt club
on horseback with baying hounds—all working
their way over the same old stones, ever-growing
in the ruts. From our porch in evening, shadow
swallows Miller's hillside field, across the valley

where it climbs between banks of oak and
hickory, ash and walnut. Shade takes the field
from bottom up, until the forest succumbs

all the way to the hilltop, where night resides.
With the last of the light we hear Miller

coming back from over the hill. He's been
tending timothy on the doctor's fields—where
crested nuthatch feed in the backwash
of harvest, as black snakes thread fieldstone
walls piled along the edges. A doe with

three fawns slips down through the orchard;
cock pheasant, his eyes flashed with red,
parades past the fish pond, then squawks
and lifts into the trees behind the house.
Turkeys prowl the thinned forest. Tomorrow

we'll replace the broken bolt on the hay rake,
prune grape canes and thin extra clusters,
have garden salad for lunch, and consider
Miller's hillside field anew. Evening heat expands
to hold us suspended on the porch after dinner

while darkness prepares to save us
the work of translating one more time
the rows and textures of these hills,
from reading the code sent by round bales
of alfalfa that appear three times a year.

COMING IN

First, the leaves and needles begin whispering—
while you're still on the trail through the re-prod forest,

before you've even made it to the big trees—they
whisper to you. And you may hear a hawk, or the thump

of grouse. That's what happens. You don't have to wait
for the old forest. But then you come under the big canopy.

Everything opens out; your ears can hear farther. You have to
stop for a moment; just stop and feel. That's what happens.

The whispering has moved to a lower register. You'll want
to whisper back, to listen deep. The space is far larger. You are

suspended in the immensity. Vine maples rule the understory
with their nine-fingered palms open to the dim light. Their

new bright green sings to your eyes. Slender branches
reach out like beggars, like prayers. After awhile you can

move on; the harmony quiets as you integrate, and you can
move again. The soft trail caresses your soft feet. You walk

slower now, with more attention. Subtle shafts of light
glance off fallen logs; drifts of gentle scent imagined,

then gone. You go on, down into the wide bowl, descending
among the columns, toward the river. You'll take it in

all at once—passing through, being changed. Then there will be one tree; it will call to you. That's what happens. You will

feel it inside. That might be the secret: to feel it inside.
You'll look up and the tree is massive, old as a planet.

Walk up and put your chin against the dark bark, arms
spread wide. Go ahead, feel what that's like. I dare you.

Too big to grasp, too tall to comprehend—your heart overloads
and stops measuring. Moss and great crevices converge

in a luminous teacup of sky. Close your eyes and feel
the subtle current, up and down. I'm not kidding.

On down the trail you'll come to the river—waterfalls, smooth
gravel and clear cold flow. You just got here and you've

already changed. Still, you have to make your way out.
That's what happens: someone else will go back.

CATKINS

They dangle in thousands from the hazels,
aligned by strict gravity, melodious notes
swept along a fine staff of branches invisible
against the dark confusion of February forest.

Long winter-flowers, hovering, pale yellow
with greenish tinge, their perfect profusion
sings an orderly chord—you can hear the hum
with your eyes.

      We have survived the big storm,
trees breaking beneath burdens of ice,
broken roofs, camp dinners, candlelight,
homes gone cold. We canceled gatherings,

postponed the overschedule, came back online
with stories—*how we made it through.*
Here in the heart of winter, autumn
has been carried way back in the runoff.

Harbingers of spring are still folded-in, buried
too deep to swell, awaiting any hint of warmth.
But these catkins pronounce a golden fairy light
that chants to us through the veiled drift of mist:

        steady in stillness,
        glimmer in the dark.

INDIAN PLUM

With their donkey-ear leaves pointing up
and tassels of tiny white flowers shooting down,
Indian Plum comets out of February into March.

All through the drowned and winter-broken forest
lime green lance-points slash over the wreckage
as hazel catkins fade to brown. Their bright omen

foretells trillium, skunk cabbage, and calls attention
to the Emerald Carpet, charged to rise in revolt
down the westward draws. Spring is near.

APRIL

after Tomas Transtromer's "April and Silence"

Under the quiet, April sits up
whispering swollen buds.
The shattered winter-gully
bristles spikes of grass that pierce
the rot of Autumn. A wealth of shouted
calm shines around and through
the white haze of plum blossom.

I am clothed in air, in warmth
at once forgotten and remembered.

A pair of ravens dance the onshore
breeze, spiral up to a madrona branch,
and grumble penetrating spells
that crack the world. There is more
to say than can be contained in words.
When even a drop in the ocean demands
the attention it deserves, language
sputters to silence.

OCTOBER FLOOD

Grays River, no longer a slip in the distance,
roars with intention through trees to the north,
having joined with the pond, down by the pasture,
to capture and cover miles of dry land.

On the broad sea of lowlands we watch from our porch,
cows have been stranded on each small rise,
and new homes protrude from this misplaced ocean
like houseboats unmoored, drifting away.

The surf, past dunes at the mouth of Grays River,
is booming drift logs into the wreck
of a tanker that blew ashore last night,
its rudder knocked loose by some freak of storm.

The road that we took to lay-in supplies,
though open last hour is likely submerged,
holding back passage past dips where the road sinks
from refugees wondering which way to go.

The wind howls at us, trees whip and dance;
our house seems to roll beneath us. We drift
from window to porch and back noting
sights we see changing before our eyes.

Teacups steam as we scan from our vantage,
secured by these candles. The world tips and spins,
as—quiet and patient—the doves in their dovecote
wait for morning to raise a new world

BETWEEN THE FEET OF GIANTS

Foghorns this morning question one another—
east and west across the channel,

north into the straits. From habit they continue—
with few boats to guide, no passenger ferries

sailing for Steamboat Island, Kamilche Point,
far Tacoma, or the old wharf whose pilings remain

at the head of Oyster Bay. Listen to distance—
another call sings a shape to the edge:

location of danger carved behind this curtain.
I wish we were out there parting folds,

feeling our way—wood hull cutting saltwater,
three-lung diesel thud and hum, sweaters,

rubber boots, windows wide in the wheelhouse,
tongues of fog licking in. I watch charts

and deadheads, you handle wheel and throttle.
Senses tuned to listen, we track a course

through nothing, with echoes reflected
from headlands, and place ourselves

by low moans that seep-in from outside
our floating world. Coffee in sips as sound builds

a picture of what to avoid—follow quiet
                              to open water.

FLOOD WARNING AND FULFILLMENT

Storm after storm off the Pacific poured
over the Black Hills in late November
and early December. The steady racket
of rain added up to floods on the Olympic rivers

while ocean-wide winds shoved twenty-foot
breakers ashore from Port Orford to Cape Flattery,
splintering drift logs, grinding fine sand finer.
I saw a goose splashing today

at home in the big runoff pond by the mall,
as passing cars buried themselves
in drench the wipers couldn't clear.
Solstice is here, another year layered

on the past. We weigh losses against
small gains, mistakes against lessons
we couldn't learn without them.
It all balances. Mistakes are inevitable;

and what teacher is greater than loss?
We bank the profit and sit by the hearth
as gravity drains hillsides into rivers,
and rivers carry silt in long plumes curling

into Puget Sound. A human being is fire.
We consume ourselves learning
that we started out whole. By grace we exist
long enough to remember beginning.

By morning the endless cloud cover
will be gone. Sodden ground will raise steam
teased to tendrils by the squinting Sun.
Spring will be along.   Winter now.

CREDO

Trees believe in sunlight
and groundwater. They bridge
the distance between, rising
to reach beyond themselves.
Shaped by shadows they probe
for wider stance, mine for moisture.
Their faith in wind creates flexibility,
their ponderous dance together
breeds variety, but all trees
may be one tree, splintered.
Trees believe in air
and thus it is made.

Most stones believe in density,
only a handful have learned
to float. Stones believe
in patience, and made:
time to prove their skill, water
to expose their art, and gravity
to bring weight and respect.
Stones are unconcerned with size.
It may be that all rocks
are one rock, reformed. Rock
believes in pressure, the pressure
it takes (and makes) being rock.

Flowers believe in bees and bats,
in butterflies and fur of animals.
They believe in loosened soil,
in rain, and mostly in sex. Once
a year is enough, and it may be
that all flowers are one flower,
always open somewhere,
always attractive. Flowers

believe in sweet, and feed sweetly
that they will be welcomed.
And they are. Flowers made wild
and welcome to meet their needs.

Water believes in motion
and fall—in carry and hold
when it moves fast, in release
when it moves slow.
And water remembers, as it curls
to the lee of a fallen log, eddies
behind a sandbar's hook, holds
the keel's cut in the wake
all across the bay. And
all water is one water, everywhere.
Water made sun to lift it, change
to drop it, cold to let it rest.

Air believes in penetration
and stasis, seeks it everywhere,
rarely finds it for long.
Air believes in fire, feeds it,
makes it grow, becomes
visible in the smoke it holds.
Air made grass to comb,
branches to tear away. Air
is one body wrapping all,
flooding to fill whatever
is held before it. Air believes
in motion and made us to move it
breathing in and out.

DANCING ALL NIGHT

They move this morning
as though by their own will;
light behind outlines
limbs lifting, a sway
to their long spines,
and synchrony, sometimes,
as they pause and lean.
They must hear a breathless blues,
clear and varied, too slow
for our rapid ears.

After a luminous riff that hangs
trembling over the mountain stage,
the wind knocks off
and the trees break for drinks
at small round tables.
Smoky mist drifts through,
laughter booms, the load off.
Sylvan conversation mutters and falls,
as the trees try out new limberness
in their wooden bones. Feet pliant
under the dance floor, the forest
shakes off long-standing torpor.

JUNGLE

Caught between the crowns of two great
mahogany trees, way out at the tippy
fine branch-ends, where leaves intermingle,
she hovers—having dreamt her way
into the lacy froth of foliage—
where she might plunge had she
living weight; where she could not be
if not for dreaming.

                She peeks through
toward the bole of one tree and sees
on a low branch, a great tiger crouched,
looking up toward her, and past. Turning
to look into the other tree, she can see
a thin man, naked, way up looking down.
Oh how intent the tiger staring up;
how fearful the shivering man.

                But then (as she watches)
something shifts in the man, something
noble rises in him (she can see it.) He sheds
the shakes and stands upright, facing-down
the orange and black magnificence
of fangs and claws. The tiger's eyes twinkle,
and the tiger sets back ready on tensed
haunches, cocked to spring.

                The man crouches
and leaps from his high perch diving
straight at the beast below, just as
the immense cat launches with a growl
toward the diving man. The two (she
calculates) will meet within her hovering
body—which they do. And she awakens,
never to be the same.

CROW CALL

A crow with something important to say
calls hard from the schoolyard. He manages
a quizzical urgency I can only dream of.

I've been in my cage all morning
storing my call in symbols on paper.
It seems important, but isn't.

The crow is *being* too well
to know it. To capture his tone
I'll have to stop *knowing*.

The crow has found food enough
to live a long life, spends his day
finding more. He says *HERE* again

and again. And he is. So much crow-calling.
I do not envy him. The world whirls
and the crow and I whirl with it.

When I die, the universe will cease, count on it.

Listen—now there are two crows.
They know they are the whole world,
and call to one another across the playfield.

It is prayer; it is song. I write some more;
the crows go to look for more food
that each world may carry on.

TEMPLE

In the cathedral made by the lifting of sky
and holding of sky, and the sky handed
from generation to generation

by trees that grew in the long shade of their elders—
thin, bean-pole trees, with branches
only at the top thread their way up until

an old one groans, gives in, and tips
its root mass as it falls, to open a flood of light,
a hole to the sky that lets the children take

the full weight of sun-food, and make themselves
finally great. Meanwhile at the floor,
salal and holly crouch with cone and fungus,

and praise the remains of light filtered down,
as they crowd along faint trails walked
by elk, black bear, now and then cougar,

and the black tail deer that feast in spring
on precious trillium. Roughed grouse thrum
from the brush, and strut with spread tailfeathers.

Among the columns scattered
under high green mist, and
the pickup-sticks of fallen trees

like ruins of ancient cultures,
alders rise, green smoke, after
a burn and dissipate almost as fast:

this blessed place knows more than you.
Step through any door onto the mossy carpet;
lean back in the crevice between the knees

of a cedar older than any country, older
than anything else you know: this place
has the tools to take you apart. You may

want to run at first. You'll want the familiar
spells that have held you in stasis. You may
wonder if—when the holding lets go—

there will be anything left of what you've come
to think is you. Be assured: for those brave enough
to remain, there will be gifts.

Silence, here, and eagles that waft their shadows
in circles cycling dark across the deep green of fir.
The lone heron that drops with a backstroke,

dangles his long limbs onto a stone
by the incoming tide to await sustenance.
The bowling ball boulders you have to dance across

in the dark to come to the phosphorescent water full
of fallen stars that trace the sweep of your hand
and the lap of every wave. Step into the explosion

of your own constellation on the sand
each time you place your foot. Twelve-armed
starfish, the low-tide clam fountain,

seven vultures circling so high they are almost
out of sight—everything here guides you to yourself.
You won't like all you've made, even though

you had no choice. But as the armoring bark sheds,
and as you sweep out daily, a bright core,
immutable, will come to light. Because you have

remained, because you have said no for now
to society, and let yourself weep for no reason,
and leak and spill, and be afraid—because wind

and rain forced you to fold inward, into darkness
so black you might have been blind, because "you"
dissolved and the real you remained, a new light spills

from your eyes. The temple, the whole landscape
has folded itself into a new realm, inside your chest,
behind your eyes and ears. And you will have this
always with you.

SIX RIDGE

Rain all day for two—wet
in wet clothes. Boots churn
with each step. Eight miles in
up steep switchbacks, the old trail
woven over around and through
dozens of new windfall trees.

Skylined on the rollercoaster ridge;
rivers in fog call from far below.
Cougar and bear crap. Primordial
landscape so rough we sleep
on the path. In the morning
a crack in the clouds lets a slice

of light into the forest. I move
to wear that warmth on my face.
Old trees and huckleberries remain
wholly still, arrayed in mantles
of diamond raindrops.
After exhale, before inhale

two birds call back and forth
across the knoll top. One swoops
a scintillating arc through the light.
Now I can't remember
how I ever thought I could be
anywhere else.

Swallowing the World ◆ Don Freas

IN THE SHOP

The chop saw had needed attention
for many months. The fence
was crooked, the stops were off—
locks barely locked, and slipped.
We all made reasonable cuts
on the thing, but we knew, too,
the old machine could cut better.

Today Tony gave in. On his own time
he stripped it down, greased
all the mating surfaces, tuned up
and tightened the springs.
He redesigned the fence, relined
the bed. The rebuild took all afternoon.
Tony smiled as he hit the switch and put

the shiny dinosaur back to work.
He turned out compound miters
that fit like glass on glass for half
an hour—until thick white smoke
poured from the motor vents,
and the whole beast blossomed
into one final exhale of flame.

YORK NARROW TAPE

Too young for Viet Nam, four of us, still boys,
were hired to clean up around the tapestry mill.
All June and July we painted, and cut back weeds,

waiting for the August holiday when the whole
place shut down. With the weavers gone
we had the factory to ourselves, and a week

to bring down greasy lint from the beams,
and from the cast iron carriages of the looms.
Supervision was slight; we climbed among miles

of taut thread, gathered from thousands of spools.
Our movements seemed large in the cathedral stillness.
We worked the odd silence and made it our own,

knocking the wood handles of our brushes against
the heavy iron of loom frame, and I-beam.
Felted lint rained in clumps and ragged sheets

to the concrete floor, past boat-shaped shuttles,
and the quiet strands made endless with tiny
weaver's knots. When the machine operators

came back they knew we had been changed.
We had seen their looms from above, and they
respected us for that. We had made it through

the quiet of their noisy realm, and knew them better.
There was pride in the silent blessing of their eyes—
as they retied threads we'd broken, as the big boiler

huffed up, and motors wound to speed, as clutches tightened and grabbed to throw shuttles through the yawning warp, spinning out clean new yards.

THE ONE YOU'RE USING

As the welding instructor shows us
the stationary grinder, with two
eight-inch high-speed grind-stones,

he calls it "the most dangerous tool
in the shop." I look around.
I see heliarc welders big as refrigerators,

slip-rollers, punch presses, hydraulic
shears that slice one-inch steel plate
like butter. We have lathes, milling

machines, and plasma cutters, a big
oxyacetylene rail cutter. With so many
options for removing clever fingers, even

whole arms, for smashing toes, and taking out
irreplaceable eyes—I'm thinking, "dangerous?
Yes. But most dangerous? In this place?"

With forty years working machinery,
I think I know better. Jim rocks the switch,
waits as the wheels wind up, and with those

wise hands slides a blank of burred steel
against the stone. As a spray of sparks
fans out, the other hulking machines recede

into gentle repose far away. From behind
safety glasses, Jim talks us through
fairing ten edges and eight corners,

then hits the switch and steps back—
all in one piece. As the grinder coasts
to rest, he guides us over to the drill press,

changes out the bit, and clamps
his well-dressed hunk of steel in the vice.
With one thumb on the switch he pauses,

looks at us, dead serious, and says:
"Watch out for this one. It's the most
dangerous machine in the shop."

AFTER THE DELUGE

Robert monkeyed the ash tree off the barn roof
where it had fallen hard, tipping roots and all, during

the Mother's Day storm. Branches punched half a dozen
holes in the corrugated tin, but the old hickory rafters

and purlins held, and are sound. We laid the upended
stump back down onto the rocky slope; the logs will go

for lumber, limbs for firewood. In Muddy Creek
we reset the pipes that keep the pond full; the fish

look happy for the fresh flow. The goslings
we hadn't seen since the flood, showed up

on the pond this afternoon; we had worried a week
that they were lost. We can comb some of the drift

away from fences and brush, and new grass
will fill in where the sod was scrubbed back,

and rolled, along the creekbanks. But the stream
has sidled off from its bed and doesn't look right

twice as wide in places. Damage from the deluge
will be with us until it seems like things have always

been this way. It'll take time. Toby will fix the roof
next Wednesday; county road crews

have been hauling the road back into place.
Noah was on his tractor down in the bottomland

by Black Swamp, plowing, when he flushed out
a new fawn, still wobbly on her fresh legs.

We saw her looking stronger the next day
at dusk along the woods. Noah planted the corn

this morning, and we'll be watching for a hint
of green on the old rocky soil. Things are looking up.

IN THE SANGRE DE CRISTO

The stones hold the memory
of water flowing and will tell you
the story when you listen.
Sometimes it's so quiet you can hear
a breeze rippling over the shell
of your own outer ear,
or the crystalline whoosh
of raven's wings. Sometimes
you can gather no sound at all.
It may not be a relief at first.
Coming here from town the peace
may seem too strange. After a while
these silent moments will be precious.
You may find yourself mining time
and the landscape for quiet, though
you'll find that even here you
have to wait. Wind, a train, birds
and squirrels keep their own counsel;
and the dips that carry silence
are easily lost as they slide through.
Pay attention—the story is long.
You can catch a few words
every day.

WARDROBE

Make me a shirt of tundra with sky filled lakes
and arctic terns in flight feasting on mosquitoes—
a boggy, watery green and blue—empty,
flat, impenetrable, endlessly attractive.

And a coat of the Canadian Rockies on an October evening
with the first dusting of snow, and vees of geese overhead.
The sun must be low in the west with mountains bowing;
the high lakes can be paint-green and choked with glacial ice.

Add a vest the patchwork pattern of clearcut
hills in Western Washington, with fanning choker trails
and switchback roads. I want beaten logging trucks
for buttons, and a piping of mud-clogged mountain streams.

Clothe my legs with two forks of a trout stream—
wild, splashing, icy clear—laced through mountains
to the sea, with pools and rapids and rocks. Let one leg
break into a waterfall, the other fill a potent reservoir.

And cobble me shoes of coastal islands with high rock soles.
Tie them with sinuous shoreline roads.
Put eagles in aeries choosing rabbits for lunch,
and Winnebagos swaying side to side in search of solitude.

Wrap a scarf of wheatfield around my neck, with a fence-
row hem and a thrumming crop duster arcing up to turn.
Work in a brace of combines, staggered, on the other side,
and a boy with his first rifle poking along a creek.

Top it all with a cloud cap, a bristling midwest
cumulonimbus thunderhead rising impossibly
over the plains, with a jagged lightning feather,
and a curtain of sweeping afternoon rain for a brim.

CLOTHES HORSE

The mannequin looked so real inside the entrance
to the restaurant, I said hello before I noticed.
Since I'd gone that far, I asked what she
was doing that evening. She said nothing,
so I suggested we do nothing together.
She accepted, so I lifted her, and carried her out.
On the way her wig fell off, and her reaction
clued me that I was onto someone special:
she wasn't embarrassed at all about her bald head,
and that ease—acceptance of herself—made her
even more beautiful to me. I retrieved the wig,
while she waited in the car, stiff as a post.
I complimented her on her stamina, and she
seemed pleased, saying most guys were always
telling her to relax. I thought about suggesting
a walk, but didn't want to carry her too far.
We went for a drive to the overlook, where
she enjoyed seeing the whole town at a glance.
We worked out where the restaurant was, among
the city lights, and I felt a shudder go through her.
We hit the dance, later, and stood around
making fun of the dancers. I felt the longing in her,
but didn't know what to do. She was a good listener,
and after a few drinks she opened up. She had a dry
sense of humor I found hilarious; we were cutting up
all over the place. I was enchanted—she was
so elegant, so statuesque. Life's hard knocks had
formed her into a solid person. It was her idea
to come to my place, for poems. We had tea
and poetry and she asked if she could stay.
I liked the idea. Climbing in bed together
was natural, as if we'd done it a thousand times,
and still appreciated the opportunity. It felt
like we had started a relationship with legs.

Swallowing the World ✦ Don Freas

I watched her fall asleep in a moonbeam.
She looked as cool laid out as she did upright.
Long-standing tension seemed to melt away
into the mattress, and I felt honored; and the next
morning I remembered how much I missed
having someone to wake up with.

WARNING

It's not your fault
It's April

You will be captured
outside the door

where an old madrona limb
reaches close to nose level

serving white arbutus flowers
that exhale soft tendrils

of delicate perfume
adrift day and night

in that oceanic
spectrum of scents

somewhere between rose
and honey

Should you lose track
of your purpose

and remain enchanted
on the porch

do not be concerned
I know about this

I will find you

Traveler

THE LETTER COMES TIGHTLY FOLDED

So you leave its labyrinthine
folds, and rest in the mystery
of your blessed life, knowing

from experience that no experience
of knowing could outweigh
its potential. Science knows as well

that acceptance of the unknowable
focuses the will, and blessings
of knowledge will flow wildly

from unknown territories. It doesn't matter
what's written, only that something is.

Our work is to unfold folded things—
we'll see what happens.

THROUGH THE NIGHT
(in two voices)

Was that you today? The heat
that blew open blossoms, unfurled new leaves,
and laid a great banquet for the green people?
Did you whisper to my grateful skin
in the garden, and leave the house warm
well into night?

> If I am the feeding sunlight, you are the star,
> you the gravity gathered in mass
> that holds me hard enough
> to crack the nut of my finest structure,
> and release me. In you I become what
> bathes planets in warmth, and reaches
> ten million millennia in all directions
> to wink at anyone who sees, anywhere,
> and ask for you. Everywhere I go
> I watch for your beholding gaze,
> everywhere seek your presence.
> You knew me! Say it!

I knew you, yes, and I drank you
for a long moment this evening
when you were the orange gilded
on the sunward side of the buxom
evening clouds. I wanted my hands
on your curves, I wanted them
to come away wet with liquid fire,
to run down my forearms in tendril flows,
and drip into the poppies and between
my toes. You let me have that—
thank you.

If I paint the clouds at evening
and clothe the nasturtiums in molten gold,
you are the flowing curves I wrap
and stroke, working my way into each crevice,
following as you roll and fold.
Before you know you have changed,
I have coated your new fullness,
shaded your hollows.
Did you think I would fail to admire
and highlight each tuck, each
smooth troweled mound?
Whatever form you choose
I arrange myself to clothe your beauty.
If you were not here to catch me,
to make me lovely,
I could not come to rest.

But when the Sun sank you left the clouds
to their darkening. I saw you leap
to settle your milky brilliance
on the moon, past half tonight,
already high as the blue drained
from the sky. We both watched
as tall conifers leaned west looking
as long as they could at their lover,
then turned toward the eastern door
to await his return. I watched you slip
silently behind the veiling clouds
in your tipping cup. Was that your gown
trailing over the bay, silver bridge
from my feet to you? I didn't know
how to cross.

My veil has always been your bridge.
You wonder how to set foot on that
watery way, how to Jesus-walk across.
Listen, what you see is not a road, waiting,
but a trail worn by passage: thousands
of diamonds—my footprints, left
while crossing again and again to you.
Have I ever failed to come to your call?

When the moon went down, I couldn't
see you. I took the drum and pushed
a long beat into the open air. You
came quickly and set my hands free,
piling the hand-strikes high
in towers of Babel, that collapsed
into elegant landslides, and built again,
while you spun from the dark hollow.
The ground barely knew the touch
of your dancing feet. The waves
of the ebbing tide showed
through the undulant flow
of skirt hung from your fluid hips;
and your hands held the world together
for another hour, two, as you held me
with glimpse of knee and thigh,
potent curve of stepping arches,
long fingers and toes.
You threw back your head and gave me
the perfect line of your throat.

You felt freed; I am grateful.
But if not for the calling of your hands
on skin, I would be aimless, wandering.
I dance from the womb-hollow

of the drum; I flash for you my lithesome thighs
so you will drive the beat. Your clever hands
sizzle the smoking hide, each strike
and slap a burst that widens in the air,
like a stone thrown in water,
demanding again that I find
whatever openings you have left vacant,
and fill them with my feet, my hands—
this prance, this wave, the only arm-thrust
that fits between the boa chains
you weave around me. Response
to your impulse, I become,
in answer to the spaces you leave,
and shatter into beauty
like a river that finds
the top of a cliff, and falls.

When finally the madness wore me out,
we fell tangled to the floor—
heads to ankles, arms lost. Damp
with sweat we bled into the rugs,
the floorboards, down into the dirt,
where I slept while you, restless,
fed yourself as spring water to fennel
and fescue, to the ancient horsetail.
You rouged the roses and moistened
the purple lips of graceful night-closed iris,
then fell asleep as the black-eyed doe
curled for an hour in tall grass
by the chuckling fountain, releasing
the breeze to fall gently down the slope,
to spill over window sills and pour
through portals, clinging in eddies
behind the doorposts. How you touched

my ears and moved my hair!
How you carried the fever away!

Without you, how could I be known?
I soaked into the ground to carry you.
I know you felt the lift of my ninety-nine
hands and ninety-nine feet, flat against
your back, under your hips, cradling
your head and neck. You stretched out
spread-eagle on my palms and soles.
With toe undulations I kneaded your
shoulders and thighs, as you drifted
from dream to dream.

With such patience you lifted your skirts
this morning, to bring up the light.
You woke me in time to stand with you
and be counted among the living,
as your first lick peeked over the hills.
When the whole orb had cleared
the ridge, and hung free, you placed
one hand on my chest, and pushed me
back to bed for one more silken hour,
while your laughter dried the dew
and drove the crows back to action.

I watched as you rose, later,
to find the iris already open,
and every broad leaf of maple
and alder already turned to face you.
We all breathed, wholly alive,
grateful for the night, and you.

SIDE DOOR

This time we come in a new way
beneath the high cathedral roof of the forest.
A woodpecker's distant tap calls us
off the road. We break through brush and climb
over fallen trunks to find this hidden sacristy.
Great columns uphold the arching sky
with their fat toes sunk in the thick green
carpet of moss. The delicate hammering
leads us to a circle of standing-dead trees.
From their shed-bark base we hear water running,
and look out across a deep valley that drops
to the ocean. Among the murmured rituals
around us we hear trillium prayers,
maidenhair prayers—the one with the line about
light from above, the one in the distance
that whispers *show me the way.* Here is the prayer
of vine maple bud, of hovering bee, and berry blossom.
We drop to our knees for the prayer
of red racer that strokes a painted line
through the loose duff, striking a clean accent
beneath the moment. Now the woodpecker
knocks again from farther in. Already lost,
we answer the call.

CHARGE

*I want to be with those who know secret things
or else alone. –Rainer Maria Rilke*

There is one thing only you can know,
      and you must

Find it. What it means that light shatters
      on moving water,

Or how the soft leaf unfurls each spring
      from the hard bud.

To find it, listen—you'll be drawn
      to the sound of boulders

Rolling under flood, or the still calm
      of black-legged

Maidenhair fern, along a mile of trail,
      in a forest, soon

To be cut for timber. You'll hold it,
      your important secret:

The smile of a child that rings
      every heart. Proof

That this is all draped over something
      out of reach—

Call it dark matter, dark energy: we can
      know, in reflection

On what we perceive and feel—the particular
      arrangement of driftwood, or stones,

On a single stretch of beach; the way to forgive
rape, murder, or war.

It will seem so necessary you'll want
everyone to see it—

It won't matter when they can't. You'll stand
on your own faith.

Wrap it in a beautiful cloth, keep it in a good box.
This is not a test;

You can't get it wrong. Take your whole life,
seeking.

We will be more than we were
before you.

MOTIVATION TECHNOLOGY

Your next car will have an engine powered
by feelings; emotions will turn the wheels.
The first wave was single-source: anger drive,

grief drive—vehicles that ran on fear, or
romantic attraction. Few humans could sustain
a single emotion long enough to get anywhere.

Most of us are more complex. We might
head out riding a burst of self-righteous hate,
then halfway down the block we feel guilty,

and drop into shame. Those motors lost power
with each shift. Put two passengers in the car,
and complexity went through the roof.

The holy grail of e-drive became a processor
that could sort and harness all emotions present
with no hesitation. Thousands of engineers grappled

with the problem. It was a freshman statistics student
from Winnipeg who figured it out. She's rich;
and reliable e-drive is coming your way.

The unforeseen side-effect will be a massive uptick
in self-awareness—you can't hide from e-drive.
Every emotional state is visible on the dashboard,

and they're all equally useful. At first, we will be
uncomfortable so exposed. Denial, shame, fear,
and blame will carry the groceries. As defenses

fall away, full exposure becomes a relief. Revelation
leads to acceptance, and we will no longer waste
energy on pretense. Contentment will arise

as a prime mover. We'll be driving
toward freedom,
for free.

THE HEART IS AN ENGINE

The fuel is fire, and stones that call out
to be stacked. The fuel is sand, made
by rivers and spread by time
along the edges of oceans,
where we walk, talking of things
important only to us. The fuel
is vast forests, roots of blackberry vines;
the fuel is the one never-grazed canyon
on the whole Colorado plateau.
The fuel is wind, waves, earthquakes.
The fuel is phosphorescent dinoflagellates
that mimic stars in the surf-chewed
seaweed churn, at the edge of Desolation Sound,
on a still night under a rusty half-moon,
at three A.M., when you can't sleep and use
the opportunity to visit the dark.
The fuel is the laughter of children,
their tiny hands and round cheeks; the fuel
is their tears—tears of loss and longing,
freely expressed—the key we forgot
and rarely remember. The fuel is kisses: stolen
kisses, little kisses, fat wet kisses. The fuel
is a glance, a long look returned, a smile.
The fuel is a glass of red wine by a warm hearth,
an empty page before you that remains unfilled.
The fuel is a braided river in full flood,
that two friends struggle with arms linked
to wade across, when her lover, his friend,
is dead. The fuel is the two of them standing
cold on the far shore knowing
they have to cross back. The fuel is hunger;
the fuel is hate. The fuel is the long road,
the first step, tall trees bending in the wind,
dancing above as you try to sleep

through a storm. The fuel is your father
growing old. The fuel is a banquet attended
by old lovers. The fuel is always volatile—
exposed to air, it quickly sublimes to vapor
and hovers in a drifting cloud that aches
for any spark. There are sparks everywhere,
and the fuel, igniting, flows fast and hot
through ports and channels into
the four-chambered cauldron, where
it burns under immense pressure,
and pushes, pushes, pushes
until everything is gone.

SCRAPYARD

When the truck drivers go on strike
we get a reprieve from loading. Most
of the yardrats use the time to work
on their hovels. We all have set aside
choice elements—like rusty Ford fenders,
round propane tanks, bent crane booms,
brass portholes with umpteen coats of paint.

So in the downtime we scramble to cram,
bend, and re-form hoarded treasures into
shack walls, foot stools, screwball cupolas,
and oil stoves. One guy is making
a bed out of wheel rims from tractors,
mattress made of car seats. Even on
days off we live and breathe scrap metal.

When the drivers settle, everything goes
back to normal. With blistered hands we
sort scrap, rattle our bones breaking scrap,
reel out long days loading the ten-yard
trucks full of scrap. They haul it all somewhere,
dump it, come back empty. The purge
never lasts: pickup trucks, beat up trucks,

dozens of rusty trucks always bring more.
The yard boss weighs the offerings, pays
by the pound. The scrappers stuff
wadded bills in torn pockets, clatter away.
We sort by metal type and set aside
what might be useful as is. Lots of so-called
artists come in. At night we crawl

Swallowing the World ◆ Don Freas

into our tin shrouds and dream of gears,
bent angle iron, golden-red rust—
everything hazed in the sweet scent
of grease. We awake each morning
to the thud of iron on iron, and roll out
for the same slug of porridge, same black
cup of mud, today's same hungry trucks.

SCENTENTIA

Clay or cardamom, saffron in the market
beside long vanilla beans—decaying fruit
tossed behind the stand. I used to avoid
the smell of compost, but now it puts me
on the road to Campuan, on Bali,
where fruit sellers bring jungle produce.

The scent of horses takes me to Anne's ranch,
her string of Fjord ponies, hot spring steam
under driving rain. I had a girlfriend
in high school I could track through the halls
by the scent of her perfume.

Betsy says the most important thing
is you have to love the man's smell
to marry him. Scent changes, though,
as love does: when you long for it,
she has you, and you are saved.

Susan said peonies smell the way
women ought to but don't. I said
we should propose that for next time.
I thought men should smell
like the memory of cherry smoke,
like a boy waking early at grandfather's cabin
to scrapple frying, shotguns gleaming
blued steel and polished walnut,
like pheasant waking in the fields,

where his uncle stroked them to sleep
at dawn, head under wing, nestling
fat birds one by one in high grass
between harvested corn fields,
along the edge where the creek

pours liquid glass over old stones,
near the copse of scrub oak
standing out from the main body
of Pennsylvania pine forest—

like a boy grown old, taking in
the scent of his wife in the morning
before she's ready to rise—her neck
drawing him for another draught
on which to build one more day.

WAKING, AS IF ALONE

I want to close today rather than open, and die—
spending my fragrance as I will.
Your beckoning continues, though, so I rise
and tour the caverns, probing shadows with my staff.

But all the caves in the honeycombed cliff-face
are empty—dried blood. As I embrace this
vaporous solitude, the fountain of silence shrieks;
my ravings await redemption, ridiculous in jewels.

Just a glimpse of the light shining through the slit
of your loosened robe, merely a hint
of intoxicating rose-scent, and all my senses knew
they would seek your inverting curves everywhere.

Why settle for breathing this love?—I've heard you moan,
lifting your nectar to my lips, begging
to be penetrated, to have your edges and entrances
traced again and again.

Why continue this fragile bridging of distance?
ANSWER ME—before I am drawn thin and dry
as a harp string, capable of only one note—mute, waiting
to be plucked again to song by your graceful hand.

PRODIGIOUS

(in two voices)

You fill my cupped hands to overflowing
and before I can dampen my thirst
most of your sweet water has spilled
between my incontinent fingers
into the unquenchable dust. Still
you offer more, tip your pitcher again
even as the last offering splashes our toes.
You know I will waste the greater portion
of this cup too, and yet you pour, then turn
for another trip to the spring. I don't know
why you remain. Surely someone less prodigal
would cherish more highly your gifts,
would deliver all the water to his lips,
halve your work to prove himself worthy
of your copious ministrations.

> Pull your hands away as I pour;
> spill it all! Lick the final drip
> from my pitcher's rim. I'll bring more.
> There was a time I suffered your
> careless lack of thrift. But you
> have taught me an abundance
> that celebrates our gifts. This dust
> is quenchable. And look at these
> unimaginable gardens arisen from
> the overflow you have caused. Spill more
> and what wondrous seeds may crack
> to spill their life into root and blossom,
> branch and leaf? Let me take myself
> to the well all day. I am prodigious
> because you are prodigal; without you
> I could not have known the depths
> of my well.

FALLING

One stride beyond
and when I look back
the door is gone. No
handhold to reach for,
nothing familiar visible
in any direction.
I thought I was
standing at the top
of a waterfall,
at the brink
where the river tips
and first realizes
what's coming.
Then you look at me,
offering everything,
and I remember
I've been falling
forever by your side.

SWITCH

I wore the burgundy taffeta gown my mother
made for my sister—who had rejected it as "too stiff
and icky." Kate said she wouldn't be caught dead in it.
So I said "Someone has to be the girl in this family."
Hell, at fifteen I was skinny enough to get into her clothes.
Katie was seventeen, and driving, so on the way
to the wedding she pulled over. While I prepared
to be bridesmaid, my sister slid her long legs
into my powder blue tuxedo pants, winding
the cummerbund over the ruffled shirt.
Shit, we looked enough alike back then we imagined
no one would notice—there was only the hair problem:
my short curly frizz, her ironed folk-singer drape.
We didn't care. We came in
stunning the crowd and Christ, acting
as if we didn't know what they were talking about.
Mom was on to us quick and hushed
our explanation that big sister's marriage
didn't have legs. She hauled us into the ladies' room
and blocked the door while we conformed to gender norms.
It didn't make a bit of difference in the grand scream of things—
what happened later would have happened anyway.

SOME ASSEMBLY REQUIRED

In the hayloft we find parts
in a crate. Some of them fit
together, and there are bolts
to hold them. In the tool shed
there's a wrench that fits
the nuts, so we tighten them,
not too much. More parts
in a box in the corner,
and hanging on nails: rods
and gears, gaskets and shims.
This appears to fit with that,
and the assembly from the loft
could fit on top. There's a whole
transmission; more tools
in a dusty toolbox. Under
a board, there's an engine block;
the crank turns. We're not
mechanics, but here we are
making an engine from
a barn full of disparate parts.
Will it fit under the hood
of the old red ragtop
under a tarp in the corncrib?
And will it run? I have doubts.
But this is what we have
to work with; and if it does,
we'll raise a fine rooster tail
racing home.

CROSSTOWN

I sat across from her in the long seat behind the driver
as the 43 bus pulled away from Fifth and Broadway.

At Sixth she suddenly said "DON'T PUSH ME DWAYNE."
toward the driver. He didn't respond, but stopped the bus

to pick up a single passenger, about seventy-five. He glanced
at her bus pass, closed the door. "And don't give me no shit

about these six-packs," the woman said, quieter.
She had four six-packs in plastic sacks at her feet.

The driver signaled a wide right turn, and his hands circled
the big wheel taking us onto Fourth. The bell sang

and he discharged passengers at Mission and at Main.
The woman let silence live all the way to the University,

then interjected—"I know what you're thinking but
you can forget it, after the way you've treated me."

The driver didn't even shrug, opened the door
for an old man at the park, who worked his way

slowly up the steps, fed a dollar into the fare machine.
The new rider took one of the handicapped seats, and the driver

pulled away from the curb. The woman said "I bet that old man
could beat the crap out of you, Dwayne." The old man frowned,

but the driver merely braked behind three cars already stopped
for the light at Jefferson. Two blocks later the sixpack lady

quietly pulled the bellcord, gathered her bags,
and got off without saying goodbye.

HALF MADE WHOLE

What can you do when
the language itself speaks
with a forked tongue?
                    Better silence

than any solution spelled out
in strings of stingy words.
There must be a sacred language,
                    long lost to us.

It has a word that says *lost-*
-and-found at once, and a term
that combines *right* with *wrong*.
                    Immersed, as we are,

in this ocean of wagging half-tongues,
we need whole words to float us home.
It's time to heal the two-sided mouth.
                    Imagine a word

that says *love-and-hate*, or *rich-*
and-poor. These unified polarities are
more real than the shallow dichotomies
                    we fabricate to justify fights.

Say *victim-and-perpetrator* in one word.
It's a paradox, yes, but so are you.
Lean in; try this: step outside
                    the barricaded self,

accept the challenge to
pull together and pronounce
the one perfect word that means
                    me-and-you.

COAL FROM SEAMS UNDERWATER

Black as the coal I lift from the beach
to sell in town, miles behind me—
the crow changes shape, turning to shadow,
and fades into cracks between breezes.

Cold, the crow dips, flying east through the light,
wind slipping over his feathers;
he lands with a lift and stroke of wings,
pushing back on the wind he comes riding.

His feet grasp the snow-coated rib that protrudes
from a twisted moose carcass remaining
beached through the high tide storm last night,
that raised coal from seams under water.

Shoulders upraised, eye cocked for motion,
the crow picks at scraps, then watches;
dry meat in his beak, hard eye scanning all,
he seems content eating alone.

You'd think he'd stand out, a crow on the snow,
picking clean what supported a life,
but he places himself outside the scene;
his call seems to come from nowhere.

I hammer a block of coal I've found;
and shatter it, scattering pieces.
I gather the chunks into the truck
topping a load by eleven o'clock.

Not bad for a day with the wind from the East
when the current heads out toward Russia;
five miles down the beach, eighty bucks in the back
for a load black as crows, fuel for fire.

WEIGHTLESS

An old boat is beached
at the meander line,

stranded when the last
high water drained away.

Surges of sea inch higher,
darken gravel, as waves climb

the steep shingle beach.
In time, lapping swells touch

the worn hornbeam keel,
work a runnel alongside

beaten wood, and begin
to ascend lapstrake ridges

of dented hull.
Dull paint brightens as the water

licks a shine. Under
the slow-chanted spell

of the ocean's rise,
the boat's dead weight

is handed ounce
by ounce from shore

to sea. One rail lifts a bit,
settles back, then lifts again.

Such a delicate ascension:
what was heavy and useless

comes alive, begins to drift,
held by the knotted tether.

But there is no boat,
no beach. My old ceramic

coffee cup has just lifted—
no less magic—from the stainless

floor of the kitchen sink.
The inexorable tide of warm water

floods from the tap
to loosen gravity's chains, take

the weight of the cup, set it free.
Grace is everywhere.

SAFECRACKER

When you're ready, slip in at night.
Avoid the alarms and cameras. Use
your talents to trick the guards.
Once you're in, the safe itself

will have inscrutable backup systems
or a combination that changes
every day. The valuables inside
were put behind all this protection

for good reason. No one could know;
you needed to forget. Survival
demanded this necessity. It was
the right thing to do. Now you are

no longer a child. You rooted out
the monster in the closet; outpaced
the bullies. The code to the lock
is etched behind your heart. Gather

your gifts; you'll need them all.
Trust yourself to adjust perspective—
you can't know what you'll find
in the dark box. With any luck

what felt life-threatening, back then,
will be simply uncomfortable now—
though when it first appears you'll
feel very small. With empathy for

the little one, spin the lock. Remember,
you were young and alone; you did
what you had to. Appreciate that—
Open the door.

BORDER CROSSING

A tree, half-fallen, arches
over the road, and someone
has tied a red bow in the center.
It seems to be a gate,
announcement of boundary,
statement of territory, and culture.
Everything changes
as under the arch
we enter a new kingdom—
strangely memorable.
Even the air is different,
and the light, as foot-soldiers,
swords raised, scramble
to line the way. The road
goes on, scattered with confetti
from last night's storm.
Our iron rims clatter
over stone as we return,
proud and humbled,
from the wars—forty years
fighting behind us, the spoils
carried home.

MANHATTAN, A PRIMER

At night in Manhattan, they crank
the buildings down, cog and pawl,
into their sockets, and roll out
Nebraska over top. Flat
grassland, bison and prairie dogs;
cowboys whoop and drive cattle.
Wide open prevails; the moon
a fat silver dollar punched
through the star-shot dark. Campfires
with harmonicas, bandannas,
singing and fistfights. Until

dawn breaks, and the big gears
ratchet all that concrete, steel,
and glass back up; everyone still
at work that never stopped.
No one noticed, but now
they can face it, in the lingering
fade of a distant dogie gettin' along,
the scattering thunder
of stampede, the high lonesome.

HOW TO HANDLE POETRY

Be wary when you encounter a poem.
You can't know by simple observation
what may be contained in that clever package:
there will be words, arrayed in puzzling forms—

contrived to appear enticing, orderly—posing
as harmless. Be advised: people have died;
civilizations have vanished. You've heard
of the Roman Empire? The Anasazi people?

How about the Soviet Union? We're pretty sure
all of these collapses were triggered by poems.
There will be more. These days most poems
are harmless. Anybody can chop up prose

and load it with emotions that say "look at me!"
Strip off the sparkles and they won't know
a paradigm shift from a stick shift.
There's so little there, most of us

ignore poems, most of the time. They offer
beguiling patterns between ads in the New Yorker,
and make us feel all intellectual as we read
a few stanzas. But this new bouncy profusion

provides devastating camouflage. You might
come across a poem and begin reading,
expecting the usual promotion for a specific
opinion, or emotional state. Without warning

the bottom falls away, and new depths unfold
in your heart. An infinite scaffolding is erected;
work begins on a towering cathedral, with
massive columns—sacred space inhabited

by angels—that invites the all-powerful
to reside within. You begin to
love more than could be healthy. It will
already be too late. Inexorably, everything

you've worked for—your entire raison-d'etre—
is relegated to the profane world outside,
along with all you recognize as you. A gate
to oceanic vastness has been opened.

Your historical activities are shown to be
pointless content filling a small corner
of the infinite context of possibility.
You no longer have any interest

in your job, consumption, TV, the personal
lives of movie stars, or politicians. You find
that the emptiness inside, that you
have been careful to avoid, has vanished.

Security becomes a joke. Borrowed thoughts
own you no longer. Before you know it, society
begins to crumble, the imminent breakup
of corporations and governments no longer

concern you. Your life unfolds into a living
crystallization of the all-possible: You'll be free!
Do not—I repeat—DO NOT READ POEMS.
The bad ones look just like the harmless ones.

The smallest can worm-in and devastate.
Better to label all poems frivolous and effete.
Just turn the page. You'll be sorry if the wrong

poem gets in. What's at stake is everything
you have limited yourself to be.
You have been warned;
take heed.

ON THE FREEWAY HOME

Several hundred yards south of the Nisqually River Bridge
I looked left to see a van, pushing a hundred, with a young
woman at the wheel, alone. She was shuttling through traffic,
weaving, grabbing any short stretch of open lane. Five cop cars
wove their own threads in pursuit, as traffic slowed
and bunched right. For the next half hour police cars trickled
out of the rearview, and were swallowed into the northern
distance ahead. The woman and her cortege made it through
the double weft of Tacoma, through the tight streams where
traffic merges at state routes sixteen and four-ten. They made it
over the tide flats at the port, up the long grade toward the airport.

For the van driver, home must have looked like not stopping
for those assholes one more time. And for all these
highly-trained professionals, home looked like stopping that van
before it tore into the knot of South Seattle and the whole city's
five o'clock fall toward dinner. Minds racing, calculating,
the procession tapped brakes, made the moves that led
to this tangled pile: the van twisted, two chase cars torn and
cross-parked in the truck lane, a parking lot of police cars with
lights flashing, traffic crawling by in the remaining lanes. News
cameras were already there; a helicopter hovered. The young
woman stood alone in the grass by the breakdown lane, hands
in cuffs, forty miles north of where she passed me at Nisqually.
Everybody was looking around; all of us trying to make it home:
no one knowing what it would take.

WILD LOVE

I know a love about leaving
  and spaces between, that allows
    moments to slip through
      and holds nothing—

a self-reliant love, grounded in passion
  that nourishes while consuming
    and finds nourishment
      being consumed.

I move toward a love that dances
  with long knives whirling
    in utter darkness
      luring me in,

a love teetering on the brink:
  nothing can stop that love when it falls,
    all that can break, will break—
      I seek that breaking,

in a love beyond names
  where what's given remains a gift,
    and further gifts
      cannot be imagined.

I know a love free of need, boundless
  in respect and fascination, a love
    always falling—true love:
      your love, of you.

Now

RAISE THE SUN

What if the Sun wouldn't rise unless you were watching?
What if all that light and heat reached all places seeking
your palms, hoping to find them upraised in welcome?

And what if the Sun, having found you attentive, having
found your open hands, could settle in and illuminate
one more day; what if you were what the Sun wanted?

And what if the light, as it fanned out toward you
and washed past you, what if that light relied
on your intention to animate form and vary color?

What if your love filled in shadow and polished
water's dance to a sparkle? Would it always be an honor
to draw trees taller and encourage shadows,

to deepen ravines with the waving of your arms?
Could you run your hands along ridges
each morning, sharpening their shape?

What if all it took was you remembering to rise,
to go out and simply bear witness to the immanent,
to just for that moment attend to the bend of climbing light,

making it rise: would that be a privilege? Could you love
enough to warm the side of a planet; would the Sun find
you waiting each day, no matter what might come?

LEAF

Look to where the veins converge—
where the leaf reaches out
from unity. Trace the branching
as it splits, and splits again, spreading,
unfurling green membranes that make
food of light. Observe the forest,
all the leaves together. Watch how wind
makes them bow, then rise. Remember
the bright greens of spring, darker greens
of high summer; watch the colors change
as winter descends. Listen to the murmur,
hear the chant: a leaf is a prayer—asked
and answered, asked again. Always
no more than that one point from which
it arose, to which it returns—
like you.

AFTER THE PAST

A little stand of redwoods holds the edge
of a meadow nearby. Ancestral winds slip

among feathery branches, and whisper
with every breath the whole history

of the world. Your story is told in there,
intrinsic, folding out—clean of analysis,

or conjecture—said fresh and wide open,
pure Being, simply offered.

Become the calm; penetrate yourself.
High branches of the great trees wave

in the wind. Shaggy bark shields
the resilience of heavy boles—so firm,

rooted in one place on the old ground.
Time may pass, but you won't know—

you won't have to. Everything
has already worked out.

ANGEL

In Valencia's Cathedral of Santa Maria,
I come to the foot of two wide marble steps
that ascend to the raised floor of the sacristy,
under the great central dome. There is no
handrail for the Spanish grandmother
who approaches from above. She looks
from side to side, wondering how to make it down.

Standing two steps below, in the promised-land
she hopes to attain, I hold out my hand and say *Ayuda?*
Her whole face opens into a smile, as the silken bird
of her right hand lights, and wraps its toes around my fingers.
I catch the word *piernas,* and know she is saying something
about her legs. With divine grace she steps down—
one step, then the other. I hear *gracias*, and remember
to say *de nada*—though in truth it means everything to me.

AT THE SCULPTURE PARK

These are brand-name works—if we don't know the sculptors,
we can recognize the donors. But we don't have to be well-read
to be moved. The world is wide open to the open. The *thing*
is hard before us: massive, flowing, giving back what we bring.
Shadows trace edges and imitate mass. Curve leads to line,
flow to wave to point and back. It all mirrors our minds. The Sun
moves and shapes change. A man with a camera weaves and
shifts as he seeks perspective, framing again what the sculptor
labored to release from the frame.

With no warning, a pack of girl-children pours across
the terraced lawn. They braid a stumbling course
that draws our attention, and brings them to light nearby.
They hold a moment, statues, trembling. Their game—
at first inscrutable—hovers, awaiting some break-out
in the shade of rusted steel. As they run on we are blessed
to gather the underlying scheme that energizes their play:
the living shape they form follows a rule of stepping
only on shadows—of sculptures, of people, of the other
moving girls. And from that abstract attempt—naïve
as it is brilliant—unfolds the perfection of all creation:
the whole majestic enterprise redeemed
as form at play gathers
to break again.

WILD STRAWBERRIES

We kept the primeval horsetail back
all spring, tearing away handfuls
of snapping canes. We watered
delicate vines as fine as hair
along with the azaleas and butterfly bushes.
Now the sugar has come in
to strawberries smaller
than peas. If we can gather
a handful between us,
I'll be surprised—
but that half-handful will be
the sweetest moment of the year.

SEVENTEEN SOUNDS OF WATER FALLING
AND THREE LEVELS OF ATTENTION

Ice remains all day in shaded puddles
housed by the first warm hours in months.
After noon a slash of light spills heat

on our faces, and throws the last
of winter in a long column downhill
through the trees. Sounds of water moving

reach us from all sides. They call out trickles,
offer draughts in pitchers, cast spells in patterns
of plunks and bloops. With a breath

we expand to the size of listening, and vanish
into the breeze. We prowl the field gathering
this hollow roll, that silver flash distinct

from the distant golden rumble. Seventeen
solos blend as we follow the lowest creases
toward the brook in the draw, and drive

on toward the bay—mingling, soaked
with laughter, singing *deeper water,*
pouring forth.

COMMITMENT

The wild silver mare sees you hanging from the low branch
and pulls the whole thundering band to run your way.

As you watch, she works her way to the edge of the pack,
picks up speed. You loosen the grip where your legs wrap

around the oaken limb, and dangle one arm. Rough bark
slips beneath your fingertips, as you gauge the vanishing

distance against imminent release. Now she is under you
and she is far too fast, and there is one slim chance—

your whole being hangs in mid air, suspended.
This is the moment; you reach, wind your whole arm

and wrist into the coarse rippling flag of her great mane.
With a handful of that fire, your body changes phase

to join her radiant field of power. Somehow you roll and slam
onto her steady back, your body a leaf tangled in her mane.

Heels reach for purchase; your chest caresses the haired-silk
rippling over her shoulders. You can't see and don't have to;

there is no need to think. She drops a few inches as she
stretches out to pour everything into speed. Together you carve

a groove in the landscape, trail a wake curling in the air.
It doesn't matter where you are going; you are under way.

DIRECTIVE

She wants to do something with lilies, something
ritual—like in May. I know it's only January
but you know she deserves it. Hell, we all do.
We need to get on with it. Give her a fast-forward,
just this once. Get her to new green, to up-thrust,

and pure white piercing the day. You owe
her this. There has been too much disaster,
too much destruction—we know too many
newly dead. Too many have become refugees;
the camps overflow with misery—

and now you want us to face winter?
Forget it. We need this. Give it one cold night—
really cold—and maybe a dusting of snow. Follow that
with a biblical downpour, something awesome,
to clear the last of the leaves. If you must you can

toss in a couple of mudslides, but only where they don't
hurt anyone. Then, by God, it better warm up—
by next week at the latest. I have no doubt you can find
a new way to complete the necessary winter folding
and unfolding, to load up the snowpack and aquifers.

We need crocus breaking ground, daffodils blown open,
the unfurling of fiddleheads. Give us the bright green
of new trillium shoots in the warm sun, lay in a spring breeze—
the whole package. We have all the gratitude in the world,
but she wants to do something with lilies.

You know you can make it happen; don't think
about it—do it. Do it now.

THE TRAIL THE CHILDREN KNOW

Sometime in this day you must rise
from work, no matter what,
and find the trail to the beach,
the one the children told you about—
through the trees, the wild trail
that begins right in your yard,
ten paces from the door;
the path past the eagle's nest,
along the maze of forest roads
that leads to where the land
meets the Sound, to where real
wilderness begins, where the push
and draw of tide is irresistible,
to where you have never been yet always
return. Sometime in this day
before the sun runs low and shades
the way, before night scrambles
the possibility, before you are
too old, before tomorrow
raises its curtain of rain
and you are dying.
             Go now;
learn the way. Bury your hands
in that cold salt-water. Live.

EXPLORATION AT DUSK

Castles and feasts, sinuous lacing roads
that comprise life and guide you
from one to the other. Lost loves,
waiting between layers of curtain;
your birthright folded in beside
the hidden exit that opens—
not to knowledge, but wonder:
your hand touching
bark and moss that touches back;
creek water flowing cold
over a forearm, until it flows through.
Shades of green overlaid
behind your eyes, wind rippling trees,
the mixture of sounds and scents
that carry your father's death with you.
A complicated cage, only small things
escape between the bars
to the Nature others have named.
Spaces between what's known,
spoken in a language no one knows,
that only you, listening, learn.

SECOND NATURE

It takes a long time, years
of practice. Make the moves
over and over—slowly
at first, then faster. Memorize
patterns, train ear and hand,
learn to play with sound
and sense. Harvest
silence from crowded corridors,
rage from empty meadows.
Drill cadences deep,
carry them everywhere.

Then, when you are threatened,
when you have to move fast,
your body will know what to do.
Motions unfold like breath,
well-worn pathways channel
the moment into song,
and—never doubt it—
making that one poem
will save your life.

DALLIANCE

The leaf that seemed motionless
has drifted from the brooksmouth
to brush past cattails and lodge
briefly in rushes. Now

it has made its way across
to linger by the upright stone.
And the lovers on the far shore
have not surfaced once.

DEADLINE

Augustus says he is out of blue, but can offer
plenty of memories, and two extra buckets
of wind. Camilla points to her surplus Cerulean,
and Gus says with a little sand he can

make that work. Camilla figures she can
mix a cup of that wind into the oversupply
of army green, and whip up a mossy froth.
They make the trade.

Clarity whispers something no one hears.
Doesn't matter: we don't have to hear it
to know she's right—Clarity always is.
We work her observation in like a secret.

White has extra weight today. It's weird.
We all avoid it because it might
go light again tomorrow, and lift everything.
Too much depends on it. We can wait.

With twelve hours to go, a small gash
opens up, and the circles go eccentric,
all but one. No one mentions it—
but a circle that ain't round shows up

like neon. Bob finishes with the barbed wire
and pulls out his silver thread.
He is incredible with a needle, so we all
breathe easier. Lick by lick, the circles

pull back to round (all but one);
we can't even see the stitches. Bob says
What else were we going to do,
paint 'em blue? No matter how much

we plan—or how much time we have—
it always comes out different,
and always at the last
minute.

NIGHT TERROR

I wake in the dark and don't know
where I am. This has been happening
since I was a child. Wherever I am,
I'm not supposed to be here.

I have no light. I don't know
where my clothes are. Waiting
until morning, until light, will only
lead to trouble, of that I'm certain—

trucks will come through and
run me down, or the tide
is coming in, or some authorized
character will find me, and mete out

punishment. It helps that there's nowhere
to turn. I've learned to hold still, quell
the urgency, and study whatever details
I can perceive: tiny points of light,

the qualities of whatever I'm sitting on,
or the dim edge of some structure.
In a moment, perspective rearranges:
the bright green planet moves

closer to become a smoke-alarm light.
The distant massive column becomes
the edge of a window. Relief arrives
with this dawn of familiarity—but also

gratitude for the other reminder—
because we don't know where we are, or
how we got here. We don't know what
will happen next, or what we will go through.

We wrap ourselves in the dramatic scenery
and align with fellow lost souls. We make up
scripts and act them out. Sometimes
we walk onto the wrong set, or forget our lines.

Sometimes we wake up in the night and—
for a few moments—suffer the truth.

AWE

Walking the perimeter
of my father's house,
inspecting for repairs, I round
the southwest corner, onto the waterside,
and there—in a patch of Florida autumn sunshine
that pours between the stately branches
of an old live oak—I come upon
a long thin whip of a rat snake, laid out,
taking the heat. The startled snake
boils up into a flailing black lariat of loops
and curves, a dancing ball of bows in motion—
holy vision—
that seers into my own adrenaline awe
as the whirling coil resolves
to vanish in an instant
through a small hole
under the foundation—
as if through a funnel—
so fast I am left
hog-tied, and branded,
as the quiet tide breathes in
through the marsh-grass.

LISTEN TO AUTUMN

If my hands move more slowly
as I age, and seem to falter,
don't think they've lost interest in form.
Taking pleasure in the spaces,

they hover in the ecstasy of making,
no longer fall toward the goal
to pronounce the loss we call success.
And if my eyes hold you too long

and go distant, it is only my fondness
for living again your beauty
through all phases. Once a moment
of conscious passion, you

have moved with grace
through ninety-nine names
to become conscious, and passionate.
And if I wander till after dark

where the tide lifts its oily mirror
doubling trees and sky
allow me time to cycle and drain.
Fed by flood, exhausted, lost,

abandoned to decay again,
I'll be found my own way.
And if I should wake before I die,
sit by me, and listen to the nonsense

I've made of thought—smuggled through,
sewn in the seams of my clothes,
as I slip past the honor guard chosen
to take me home. Have patience.

CARDS

We might get lucky or he might fire us, hard
to say. I'll take two cards. Pass the strawberries.

See your dollar, raise you two. The two migrants,
the church lady—nobody else was there. Did not

happen like she said; I knew those boys.
A misunderstanding, but funny. She got scared,

thought something was going to happen;
started yelling. But it didn't. If you could

charge people for your fears, well... See your
two, raise you two. Took three of us to talk

Carlos out of the woods. No, he went back
to Mexico. Wanted to be with his grandkids.

Outside Guanajuato. Family is family.
Pot's right. Jesús is still here; have you not

been to the hardware? He's back
in the yard.   Yeah.   Only two pair

but they beat your kings. Good thing
I stayed with it. Who'll pay a dollar

for five card stud? Now, that's another
story that has grown over the years.

I wasn't there—but I can't believe everybody
else and half their aunts and uncles were—

even people that weren't born yet. That church
couldn't hold so many. Oh you were, were you?

Then you know what I'm saying.
I'm afraid I'll have to take three.

ALL THE WRONG PLACES

No one told me you were in cars and concrete.
I didn't know to look in clearcuts and dreary alleyways.
Who would think to search the vicinity

of cast-off hypodermics, fogged plastic dime-bag litter,
to suffer the reek of city dumpsters, or consider
the torn bedroll under a sagging cardboard tent

in a little patch of littered salal and blackberries
by the park? There you were all along:
where the effluent pours out gray and sweet

under the dock, hovering pink through the night
in the caustic flare of anti-crime streetlights,
shuffled in with the parade of knife and gunshot wounds

walking and wheeling through the swinging E. R. doors.
You fight and rape and ice-pick tires.
How could I have failed to notice your clever hand

in the hopeful eyes of the beaten hound, your presence
among the predictable clump of fast food restaurants
by the gas station, your pure light from the magazine cover

on the porno rack. I thought you were dying,
or that I had lost my way to you. I was blind,
but your steady radiance has given back my eyes.

TURN

The Earth keeps turning.
                Rain, then sun.
Time stumbles on itself.
                Deserts spread as forests
dissolve and the planet
                warms. There is war
and genocide, and people
                die for lack of food.
The reasons seem clear,
                but aren't.
We arrive and travel a spiral,
                lifting ourselves
with countless dancing steps
                that rise—
maybe just a little. We want
                to live, and so
we march against
                or into war.
There is so much good
                work to be done.
So many need our vision
                and courage. And our
own lives miss us,
                going along quietly
alone.

READING MY OWN POEMS

My piss, distilled
from last night's wine,
still soaks the ground.

Every muscle is sore
from too much dancing—

Rumi and Kabir are dust,
but I will dance again, tonight.

NOW

Look around—this is it.

I'm serious, look around.

Feel into the details: the place,
the scent, the light, sound of birds
or cars, the reader's voice,
susurration of the audience,
how the air feels on your hands,
or cheeks. Here. Right now.
The whole thing. You're at
the very center of whatever
is going on. There is nowhere else
you could be, nowhere else
you've ever been. Words on a page
or in your ears. Bump something:
that's you. This is the here of now.
You have no choice other than
how to feel about it. It's the last scene.
Take it in. It's always the last scene.
This is how it all worked out.

Made in the USA
San Bernardino, CA
09 August 2016